— The will of God

BEHOLD

HIS GLORY

BEHOLD
HIS GLORY

Jesus in the Balance

- Dennis Gulliford -

TATE PUBLISHING
AND ENTERPRISES, LLC

Published by Tate Publishing & Enterprises, LLC
127 E. Trade Center Terrace | Mustang, Oklahoma 73064 USA
1.888.361.9473 | www.tatepublishing.com

Tate Publishing is committed to excellence in the publishing industry. The company reflects the philosophy established by the founders, based on Psalm 68:11,
"The Lord gave the word and great was the company of those who published it."

Book design copyright © 2012 by Tate Publishing, LLC. All rights reserved.
Cover design by Shawn Collins
Interior design by Sarah Kirchen

Published in the United States of America

ISBN: 978-1-61862-219-8
1. Religion / Christian Life / Personal Growth
2. Religion / Christian Life / Spiritual Growth
12.03.23

Dedicated to Elisabeth, Margaret,
John, Damaris, and Abigail.

I have no greater joy than this, to hear of my
children walking in the truth.

3 John 4

Let the words of my mouth and the meditation of
my heart be acceptable in Your sight, O LORD, my
rock and my Redeemer.

Psalm 19:14

ACKNOWLEDGEMENTS

You know how people refer to God and abuse the name of Jesus Christ. Do you know what God says about Himself in His Word? It is my hope and prayer that you will read the Bible for yourself and know the God of the Bible by His own Word and by faith in His Son, Jesus.

My life is marked by the God of the Bible and by His Word. To my children, Elisabeth, Margaret, John, Damaris, and Abigail, who have heard God's Word in our home from their childhood, it is my hope and prayer that you and your children will know and love God and His Word and that you will walk with the Lord Jesus on the paths of righteousness all the days of your lives.

Althea, you are my greatest blessing from the Lord. Thank you for walking with me.

TABLE OF CONTENTS

THE GLORY OF GOD

As John and the other disciples spent time with Jesus, they came to know Jesus and to believe in Him. John later wrote, "We beheld His glory." (John 1:14) Do you?

The literal sense of the Hebrew word *glory* has to do with weight. An object in a market is weighed to determine its value. The glory or weight of something in the balance demonstrates what it is and measures what it is worth. To behold the glory of Jesus is to see who He is and His worth.

To have glory is literally to be heavy or weighty. Figuratively, a weighty person is someone who is honorable; impressive; and worthy of respect, attention, and obedience.[1] Glory is that which gives weight to and authenticates and demonstrates the identity, nature, and worth of an object or person. An action or statement that glorifies God is one that demonstrates and proclaims that God is worthy of our worship, obedience, faith, hope, and love.

As you read of the promise, the Gospel, the Son, the works, the will, and the worship of God, you will find many Bible references. Do not be distracted by them or feel compelled to look them all up. On the other hand, at any point you want to see something for yourself like Thomas (John 20:24-25) or like the brethren at Berea (Acts 17:10-11), the Bible references are given as a starting point for you.

Consider the claims of Jesus to be the almighty, life-giving, eternal God worthy of our worship, that is, God the Son. Consider the Bible's affirmation that Jesus is worthy of our faith and worship. And when you see the words, "Behold His glory," take it as a personal invitation to look carefully at who Jesus is and consider how much weight He should carry in your life.

Behold His glory.

THE PROMISE OF GOD

Abraham

> ...with respect to *the promise of God*, he did not
> waver in unbelief but grew strong in faith, giving
> glory to God, and being fully assured that what
> God had promised, He was able also to perform.
>
> Romans 4:20-21 (italics mine)

Incest, murder, rape, personal and international intrigue
and betrayal, a grandma who murdered her own grandchildren, kings who slaughtered babies, battles, wars, friendship,
hatred, love, poetry, sins you would not want your children to
know about, heroics retold to children everywhere—that is
just the beginning of what you find in the Bible. If you have
never read it, the Bible is probably not what you expect.

From the beginning in Genesis to the final Revelation of
who Jesus Christ is, the central focus through all of Scripture
is not mankind or any nation or group of people or individual but God Himself (Psalm 102:18-28; 1Chronicles
29:15, 10-20; John 5:39-40). As the Biblical account of God's
dealing with mankind unfolds, the central focus of Scripture

is the revelation of the character and nature of God. We see ourselves for who and what we are in the light of the revelation of the glory of God.

Scripture begins with the Old Testament, which is the story of a promise made and kept by God. There is no greater story of faithfulness and steadfast love than this story of God's faithfulness to keep His promise. After an account of how it all began as a foundation, God made His promise in Genesis chapter 12. The rest of the Old Testament is the story of God's holiness, justice, goodness, mercy, grace, compassion, steadfast love, and faithfulness to keep His promise. In brief, this is the story of the promise of God.

The Bible begins in **Genesis** chapters 1 and 2 with an account of the goodness of God's creation (Genesis 1:4, 10, 12, 18, 21, 25, 31; 2:9, 18). The badness begins in chapter 3 with Adam and Eve and the first sin. Things went downhill fast from the first sin, as chapter 4 records the account of Cain and Abel and the first murder. Chapters 5 and 10 are genealogy, that is, lists of names and families that present the Bible as an accurate, historical record. Genesis chapters 6 through 9 are the account of Noah and the flood. Chapter 11 is the account of how God dealt with the wholesale rebellion of mankind against Him at the Tower of Babel.

As history unfolds, in Genesis 12, we meet a man named Abram. In accordance with His grace, God chose this one man from the entire human race and promised to give him three things if he would leave his country, relatives, and home and go to a land that God would show him when he got there

(Hebrews 11:8). God promised to give that land to Abram and to his descendants as an eternal inheritance. God also promised to bless him and to make his descendants into a great nation (Hebrews 11:11-12). And finally, God promised that through Abram, all the families of the earth would be blessed (Genesis 12:1-3; 22:18). As history unfolds, we discover that the blessing to all coming through Abram would be Jesus, the Savior.

God promised all this to Abram on one condition: that he believe the promise of God and go to the land of Canaan, which Abram did. Abram's faith in the promise of God and obedience to God make the fulfillment of the promise unconditional to us because Abram, by faith, fulfilled the only condition to receive the promise by going to the promised land. Whether or not God would send Jesus the promise did not depend on us but only on Abram's faith and obedience (Genesis 22:18). According to the Bible, we today have received God's promise to provide a savior no matter who we are or how we live because Abram met the condition to receive the promise.

The promise that God would send us His blessing, Jesus our Savior, through Abraham (Galatians 3:8, 14) was guaranteed when Abraham, the father of faith, believed God's *promise* and obeyed.

> For this reason, it is by faith, in order that it may be in accordance with grace, so that the promise will be guaranteed to all the descendants, not only to those who are of the Law but also to those who are of

the faith of Abraham, who is the father of us all… In hope against hope, he believed so that he might become a father of many nations according to that which had been spoken: "So shall your descendants be." Without becoming weak in faith, he contemplated his own body, now as good as dead since he was about a hundred years old, and the deadness of Sarah's womb; yet, with respect to *the promise of God*, he did not waver in unbelief but grew strong in faith, giving glory to God and being fully assured that what God had promised, He was able also to perform (Romans 4:16-21; italics mine).

After Abram obeyed God and went to the promised land of Canaan, God changed his name to Abraham. The promise went through Abraham (Genesis 22:18; Matthew 1:1). Abraham had two sons, Ishmael and Isaac. By where his descendants settled (Genesis 25:12-18) and how they lived (Genesis 37:25), it appears that Ishmael, born to Hagar the Egyptian, became the father of the Bedouin Arab nations (Genesis 16). To this day, the sons of Ishmael are still fighting the sons of Isaac for the promised land, but the promise went through Isaac, born to Sarah (Genesis 21:12).

Isaac had two sons: Jacob and Esau. Esau, who sold his birthright for a bowl of soup, became the father of the Edomites (Genesis 29:31 to 30:24; 35:16-27). The promise went through Jacob (Genesis 27; 28:10-15).

Jacob had twelve sons and a daughter named Dinah (Genesis 29:31 to 30:24; 35:16-18). In Genesis chapter

32, Jacob wrestled with an angel and God changed his name to Israel (Genesis 32:28). Through the rest of the Old Testament, the people of the promise are known as the children of Israel (Genesis 49:1-2; Exodus 32:13; 1 Kings 18:36; 2 Kings 17:34; I Chronicles 29:18; 2 Chronicles 30:6).

Israel (Jacob) loved his son Joseph more than all his sons. Joseph's brothers became jealous of him and sold Joseph to the Ishmaelites, who carried him off to Egypt and sold him into slavery (Genesis 37:3-36). In Egypt, Joseph interpreted two dreams for Pharaoh that predicted seven years of plenty followed by seven years of famine. Because of this, Pharaoh made Joseph second in command in all of Egypt (Genesis 41). When the famine came, Joseph's brothers came to Egypt to buy food (Genesis 42-44). Joseph forgave them, and the whole family, including Israel himself, moved to Egypt. Although his brothers intended it for evil when they sold Joseph, God used it for good to save His people from starvation (Genesis 45:1 to 47:12).

Israel's twelve sons became the fathers, or patriarchs, of the twelve tribes of Israel (Genesis 49; Acts 7:8). Because of the sins of the oldest three sons, Reuben, Simeon, and Levi (Genesis 49:1-7), the promise went through the fourth son, Judah: "The scepter shall not depart from Judah, nor the ruler's staff from between his feet, until Shiloh comes, and to him shall be the obedience of the peoples" (Genesis 49:10; Matthew 1:2).

The history of the **Exodus** began four hundred and thirty years after the sons of Israel moved to Egypt. (Genesis

15:13; Exodus 12:40-42; Galatians 3:17-18) At that time a new pharaoh, who did not know Joseph, arose (Exodus 1:8). The sons of Israel who came to Egypt as a family of seventy (Genesis 46:26-27; Deuteronomy 10:22; Acts 7:14), had become a nation of about 2 million or more slaves. (Numbers 1:1-47 says 603,550 men only, excluding the tribe of Levi; assuming wives and children, likely more than 2 million.) God provided a deliverer named Moses. After a series of ten plagues (Exodus 6-12), Moses led the sons of Israel out of Egypt and across the sea on dry ground. When Pharaoh's army followed, it was drowned (Exodus 14). Instead of turning north toward the promised land, because God had commanded him from the burning bush to return there (Exodus 3:1-12; Acts 7:30-38), Moses led the sons of Israel south back to Mount Sinai (Horeb), where God gave them two important things:

- the Law including the Ten Commandments—**Leviticus** (Exodus 19-20), which was God's description to them of what love looks like in practice. (See Matthew 22:35-40 and Romans 13:8-10).

- plans to build the tabernacle (Exodus 25-31), which they built at Mount Sinai (Exodus 35-39).

Numbers is the story of the journey of the sons of Israel from Mount Sinai (Numbers 10:11-13) back to the promised land (Numbers 33). After taking a census, that is numbers (Numbers 1), the sons of Israel moved north to Kadesh-barnea, where they sent twelve spies into the land (Numbers

13:1-26). Ten spies reported that the land was inhabited by giants too strong for them (Numbers 13:27-33). Joshua and Caleb reported,

> "The land which we passed through to spy out is an exceedingly good land. If the LORD is pleased with us, then He will bring us into this land and give it to us...Only do not rebel against the LORD..."

> Numbers 14:5-9

After all they had seen God do in Egypt and at Mount Sinai, the people still did not believe the promise of God and decided not to enter the land (Deuteronomy 1:25-33; Numbers 14:1-4, 10-11). For rejecting God's promise, the sons of Israel wandered in the wilderness until all those who were twenty years of age and older at Kadesh-barnea died (Numbers 14:20-38; 26:1-2, 63-65). None of those who rebelled against God at Kadesh-barnea entered the promised land. Consider the consequences of rejecting the promise of God.

After forty years of wandering in the wilderness (Numbers 14:34), the sons of Israel arrived at the east bank of the Jordan River (Numbers 36:13). There, Moses gave his farewell address, the book of **Deuteronomy** (Deuteronomy 1:1). Then Moses died (Deuteronomy 34). Only Joshua and Caleb survived the wandering in the wilderness (Numbers 26.65), and their strength was not diminished (Joshua 14:6-15).

Joshua led the sons of Israel across the Jordan River back into the promised land (Joshua 1:1-9). When Joshua sent two spies into Jericho, Rahab the prostitute hid them and helped them. Rahab confessed,

> "I know that the LORD has given you the land…for the LORD your God, He is God in heaven above and on earth beneath."
>
> Joshua 2.9-11

When the walls of Jericho fell (Joshua 6), God protected Rahab, and the promise went through Rahab, who became the wife of Salmon, mother of Boaz and mother-in-law of Ruth (Matthew 1:5). The sons of Israel conquered the city of Ai next (Joshua 7-8). Then Joshua divided the land between the twelve tribes (Joshua 13-19), and each tribe was responsible to finish conquering the land given to it. But the sons of Israel never fully completed the conquest (Judges 1:27-36) and later paid heavily for their disobedience (Numbers 33:50-56).

The period of the **Judges** followed in which a cycle of four events reoccurred repeatedly:

1. The sons of Israel turned back from following the Lord (Judges 2:8-13).

2. A foreign nation not conquered under Joshua (Judges 2:20-23) oppressed them (Judges 2:14-15).

3. When the Lord heard their groaning, He raised up a judge like Gideon, Deborah, or Samson to deliver them (Judges 2:16-18).

4. The sons of Israel followed the Lord during the life of that judge (Judges 2:19). Then the cycle repeated itself again (Judges 2:19-23). The last verse in the book of Judges is a good summary of this period:

> In those days there was no king in Israel; everyone did what was right in his own eyes *(not what was right in the Lord's eyes).*
>
> Judges 21:25 (italicized phrase added by me)

Ruth lived in the days when the judges judged (Ruth 1:1-4). The promise went through Ruth (Matthew 1:5), a foreign Moabite woman who believed God (Ruth 1:14-16). Ruth married Boaz and became the great grandmother of King David (Ruth 4:18-22).

Samuel, the last judge (1 Samuel 7:15), was also confirmed as a prophet in Israel (1 Samuel 3:19-21). The prophets were servants of God to whom He revealed Himself and who spoke in His name (Daniel 9:6, 1 Samuel 3:21). The Lord called Samuel to anoint the first two kings of Israel (1 Samuel 8), first Saul (1 Samuel 9-10) and then David (1 Samuel 16:1-13). Samuel recorded the life of King David. The promise went through David (Matthew 1:1; Revelation 22:16).

The books of the **Kings** and **Chronicles** record the acts of David's son, King Solomon, and all the rest of the kings that followed him. When Solomon died, (1 Kings 11:41-43) the kingdom was split because of the sins of Solomon (1 Kings 11:1-13) and the foolishness of his son Rehoboam. (1 Kings

12:1-15). Solomon's servant, Jeroboam, (1 Kings 11:26-40) led the revolt that split the kingdom (1 Kings 12:16-24). The ten northern tribes of Israel followed Jeroboam and made him their king (1 Kings 12:20). Only the tribes of Judah and Benjamin remained loyal to King Rehoboam in Jerusalem (1 Kings 12:21).

To consolidate his kingdom, Jeroboam drove Israel away from following the Lord and made them commit a great sin (2 Kings 17:20-23). He set up two golden calves and commanded the ten northern tribes of Israel to worship these rather than going to Jerusalem on the feast days to worship the Lord in Solomon's temple (1 Kings 12:25-33). The northern kingdom of Israel had eighteen kings, who all did evil in the sight of the Lord. Elijah and Elisha were the two great prophets to the kingdom of Israel.

When Shalmaneser, king of Assyria, invaded Israel, Hoshea, the last king of Israel, became his servant and paid him tribute. Later, Hoshea rebelled against Assyria and stopped paying his annual tribute. Assyria invaded again, and after a three-year siege, Shalmaneser captured Samaria, Israel's capital city, in 722 BC and carried the northern kingdom of Israel away into captivity (2 Kings 17:1-18).

> So the LORD was very angry with Israel and removed them from His sight; none was left except the tribe of Judah.
>
> 2 Kings 17:18

Scripture does not record that these tribes ever returned to the promised land, and they are sometimes called the ten lost tribes of Israel. However, to the prophet Jeremiah, the Lord declared of these tribes of Israel,

> I will also bring them back to the land that I gave to their forefathers and they shall possess it.
>
> Jeremiah 30:3

> At that time, declares the LORD, "I will be the God of *all the families of Israel*, and they shall be My people...I have loved you with an everlasting love."
>
> Jeremiah 31:1-6 (italics mine)

> "Behold, days are coming," declares the LORD, "when I will make a new covenant *with the house of Israel and with the house of Judah*...I will be their God, and they shall be My people...for I will forgive their iniquity, and their sin I will remember no more."
>
> Jeremiah 31.31-34 (italics mine)

God revealed more than His holiness and justice in His judgment of Israel's evil and sin. Nowhere are God's mercy, grace, compassion, and steadfast love more visible than in His promise, "I will forgive...I have loved you with an everlasting love".

Remember, the promise went through Israel's fourth son, Judah and his sons, the kings of Judah. The blessing to all, the Messiah, Jesus, would come from the lineage of King David (2 Samuel 7:16-17; Isaiah 9:6-7; Jeremiah 33:17-26; Psalm 89:3-4; 2 Timothy 2:8) of the tribe of Judah (Matthew 1:1-6). The southern kingdom of Judah had nineteen kings and a queen. Eight kings did right in the sight of the Lord (Asa, 1 Kings 15:11; Jehoshaphat, 1 Kings 22:41-45; Joash, 2 Kings 12:1-3; Amaziah, 2 Kings 14:1-4; Uzziah, also called Azariah, 2 Kings 15:1-4; Jotham, 2 Kings 15:32-35; Hezekiah, 2 Kings 18:1-8; and Josiah, 2 Kings 22:1-2). The rest did evil. Isaiah and Jeremiah were the two great prophets to the kingdom of Judah.

One of the truly great heroines of the Old Testament, Jehoshabeath, is not well known because the graphic content of her story is generally and understandably omitted from the Sunday school version of the Bible. Could you imagine a Sunday school lesson that began like this? "Today, boys and girls, we are going to hear the story of the mean grandma who murdered her own grandchildren." That's what happened. When King Ahaziah died, the king's mother, Athaliah, plotted her own ascent to the throne by murdering all the rightful heirs. In the midst of the slaughter, Jehoshabeath, the king's sister, hid baby Joash (2 Chronicles 22:10-12). Queen Athaliah came within one baby grandson of breaking God's promise. God used the bravery of his aunt Jehoshabeath to save Joash from his wicked grandma Athaliah's plot to kill him, and God kept His promise that David would never lack a man to sit on the throne of the house of Israel (Jeremiah 33:17). Jehoshabeath and her husband Jehoiada the priest hid

Joash from Queen Athaliah in the temple for seven years. (Athaliah evidently did not spend much time in the temple, worshipping God, during her reign.) Then Jehoiada led a coup of army officers that overthrew Athaliah, executed her, and placed Joash, the rightful king, on the throne at age seven (2 Chronicles 23:1 to 24:1).

A great revelation of the glory of God came through the prophet Isaiah during the reign of Hezekiah, king of Judah. After the Assyrian destruction of Samaria in 722 BC, Sennacherib, King of Assyria, brought the full weight (glory) of the Assyrian empire down on Judah in 701 BC (Isaiah 36:1).

> (Today you can stand in the Oriental Institute of the University of Chicago in front of a cast of the Taylor Prism, named after the archaeologist who found the obelisk. On the Taylor Prism, you can read Sennacherib's version of his campaign, as he recorded it on this stone obelisk recovered from his capital city of Nineveh, if you can read Assyrian cuneiforms. In one section of the inscription on the obelisk, Sennacherib bragged, "As for Hezekiah, the Jew…Himself, like a caged bird, I shut up in Jerusalem, his royal city…the terrifying splendor of my majesty overcame him." Archeology and secular history support the accuracy of biblical history.)[2]

During his siege of Jerusalem, Sennacherib sent messengers to Hezekiah with a demand for surrender that read in part:

Do not let your God in whom you trust deceive you, saying, "Jerusalem will not be given into the hand of the king of Assyria." Behold, you have heard what the kings of Assyria have done to all the lands, destroying them completely. So will you be spared? Did the gods of those nations which my fathers have destroyed (*including the northern kingdom of Israel*) deliver them…?

Isaiah 37:10-12 (italicized phrase added by me)

This implication of Sennacherib's demand for surrender was certainly understood by Hezekiah.

Then Hezekiah took the letter from the hand of the messengers and read it, and he went up to the house of the Lord and spread it out before the Lord. Hezekiah prayed to the Lord saying, "O Lord of hosts, the God of Israel, who is enthroned above the cherubim, You are the God, You alone, of all the kingdoms of the earth. You have made heaven and earth. Incline Your ear, O Lord, and hear; open Your eyes, O Lord, and see; and listen to all the words of Sennacherib, who sent them to reproach the living God. Truly, O Lord, the kings of Assyria have devastated all the countries and their lands, and have cast their gods into the fire, for they were not gods but the work of men's hands, wood and stone. So they have destroyed them. Now, O Lord our God, deliver us from his hand that all the kingdoms of the earth may know that You alone, Lord, are God."

Isaiah 37:14-20

Sennacherib bragged, in effect, "No other god has been able to resist Assyria, and your God is no different from any other god." Hezekiah took the letter; laid it out in the temple before the Lord; and prayed,

> O Lord of hosts, the God of Israel, who is enthroned above the cherubim, *You are the God, You alone* (italics mine).

In essence, Hezekiah prayed, "Lord God, this is between You and Sennacherib. I'm out of it. Lord, it is You that Sennacherib has insulted, not me."

> Now, O Lord our God, deliver us from his hand that all the kingdoms of the earth may know that *You alone, Lord, are God*" (italics mine).

There is the issue: who is God?

God did "listen to all the words of Sennacherib, who sent them to reproach the living God," and God acted:

> Then the angel of the Lord went out and struck 185,000 in the camp of the Assyrians; and when men arose early in the morning, behold, all of these were dead. So Sennacherib king of Assyria departed and returned home and lived at Nineveh. It came about as he was worshiping in the house of Nisroch

his god, that Adrammelech and Sharezer his sons killed him with the sword;

Isaiah 37:36-38

When Sennacherib reproached "the living God" God acted. So Sennacherib went back to his own home, where his own sons murdered him in his own temple worshiping his own god.

But God did more than act to show the people of the promise and all the kingdoms of the earth that He alone is God. Who is God? Through the prophet Isaiah, God emphatically answered Sennacherib:

> *I am* the LORD, that is *My name*; I will not give My glory to another, nor My praise to graven images.

Isaiah 42:8

> "You are My witnesses," declares the LORD, "and My servant whom I have chosen, so that you may know and believe Me and understand that *I am* He. Before Me there was no God formed, and there will be none after Me. I, even *I, am* the LORD, and there is no savior besides Me. It is I who have declared and saved and proclaimed, and there was no strange god among you; so you are My witnesses," declares the LORD, "and *I am God.*"

Isaiah 43:10-12

I am the first and *I am* the last, and there is no God besides Me.

Isaiah 44:6

For My own sake, for My own sake, I will act; for how can *My name* be profaned? And My glory I will not give to another.

Isaiah 48:11

Therefore My people shall know *My name*; therefore in that day *I am* the one who is speaking, "Here *I am*."

Isaiah 52:6 (italics mine in
all the above quotes from Isaiah)
(Also see Exodus 3:13-15 and John 8:58.)

He was despised and forsaken of men, a man of sorrows and acquainted with grief; and like one from whom men hide their face He was despised, and we did not esteem Him. Surely our griefs He Himself bore, and our sorrows He carried; yet we ourselves esteemed Him stricken, smitten of God, and afflicted. But He was pierced through for our transgressions, He was crushed for our iniquities; the chastening for our well-being fell upon Him, and by His scourging we are healed. All of us like sheep have gone astray, each of us has turned to his own way; but the LORD has caused the iniquity of us all to fall on Him.

Isaiah 53:3-6

Jesus fulfilled these words of Isaiah. All the nations offered sacrifices to their gods, but our God would offer His own Son as a sacrifice for us. There is no god like our God.

Who is God?

> "You are My witnesses," declares the LORD, "and My servant whom I have chosen, so that you may know and believe Me and understand that *I am* He. Before Me there was no God formed, and there will be none after Me. I, even I, am the LORD, and there is no *savior* besides Me."
>
> Isaiah 43:10-12 (italics mine)

> "…the Righteous One, My Servant, will justify the many, as He will bear their iniquities…because He poured out Himself to death, and was numbered with the transgressors; yet He Himself bore the sin of many, and interceded for the transgressors."
>
> Isaiah 53:11-12

In response to Sennacherib's reproach and Hezekiah's faith, God revealed more of His glory and of His promise to send a Savior. That promise went through Hezekiah, king of Judah (Matthew 1:9-10).

After this account of Hezekiah's faith, the evil of Manasseh, son of Hezekiah, is noteworthy. (2 Kings 21:1-18)

> Because Manasseh king of Judah has done these abominations, having done wickedly more than all the Amorites did who were before him, and has also

made Judah sin with his idols; therefore thus says the LORD, the God of Israel, "Behold, I am bringing such calamity on Jerusalem and Judah, that whoever hears of it, both his ears will tingle…I will wipe Jerusalem as one wipes a dish, wiping it and turning it upside down."

2 Kings 21:11-13

Josiah, the grandson of Manasseh, is noteworthy for his repentance.

Surely such a Passover had not been celebrated from the days of the judges who judged Israel, nor in all the days of the kings of Israel and of the kings of Judah. But in the eighteenth year of King Josiah, this Passover was observed to the Lord in Jerusalem…Before him there was no king like him who turned to the Lord with all his heart and with all his soul and with all his might, according to all the law of Moses; nor did any like him arise after him. However, the Lord did not turn from the fierceness of His great wrath with which His anger burned against Judah because of all the provocations with which Manasseh had provoked Him. The Lord said, "I will remove Judah also from My sight, as I have removed Israel. And I will cast off Jerusalem, this city which I have chosen, and the temple of which I said, 'My name shall be there'".

2 Kings 23:21-27

(Historical note: In 609 BC, Pharaoh Necho marched his Egyptian forces north to join Assyrian forces in an attempt to stop Babylonian expansion at the Euphrates River. When King Josiah tried to stop the Egyptian army's march north through Judah, plundering the land as they advanced, he was defeated and killed at Megiddo (2 Kings 23:29). In those days, armies on the march did not have supply trains. Armies deployed in the field supported themselves by rape, pillage, and plunder.

At the battle of Carchemish in the spring of 605 BC, Babylonian forces under Nebuchadnezzar routed the combined Assyrian and Egyptian armies (Jeremiah 46:2). The tactics used by Nebuchadnezzar at Carchemish were so genius that they are still studied today. Some of Nebuchadnezzar's tactics were employed by the Allies for the D-Day invasion.

The Assyrian forces that survived the battle of Carchemish fled north, virtually out of recorded history. As the Egyptian army retreated south toward Egypt pursued by the Babylonians, Nebuchadnezzar came up to Jerusalem and King Jehoiakim became his servant (2 Kings 24:1). The Battle of Carchemish has a firm date of 605 BC in secular history. Jeremiah 46:2 is the Bible verse that allows biblical scholars to synchronize biblical history with secular history. Old Testament dates have generally been calculated by counting forward and backward in the Bible from the fourth year of the reign of Jehoiakim and the Battle of Carchemish in 605 BC.)[3]

Nebuchadnezzar, king of Babylon, came up against Jerusalem three times. The first time, he robbed the temple and took King Jehoiakim and some of the royal family and nobles captive back to Babylon. (2 Chronicles 36:5-7). Daniel was taken captive at that time (Daniel 1:1-7). Nebuchadnezzar returned a second time and took everything of value he could carry, all the captains and mighty men of valor, all the craftsmen and artisans, and King Jehoiachin (also called Jeconiah, Jeremiah 27:20; see also Jeremiah 22:24 and 37:1) captive back to Babylon (2 Kings 24:10-17). When Zedekiah, who was the uncle of Jeconiah and the last king of Judah, rebelled, Nebuchadnezar apparently had had enough. After a year-and-a-half siege, Nebuchadnezar conquered Jerusalem for the third and last time in 586 BC. This time, Nebuchadnezzar had all the sons of Zedekiah slaughtered before his eyes. So it would be the last thing he ever saw, King Zedekiah was then blinded and taken to Babylon in chains. (2 Kings 25:1-7). But the promise went through the previous king, Jeconiah, in the line of David, already held captive in Babylon (Matthew 1:11-12). The Babylonians destroyed the temple, burned everything in Jerusalem that would burn (Jeremiah 32:28-29), and demolished the entire wall around Jerusalem (2 Kings 25:8-10). Except for some of the poorest of the land, all those who escaped the sword (2 Chronicles 36:17-21) were taken captive back to Babylon (2 Kings 25:11-12) along with everything left of any value (2 Kings 25:13-17).

Years later, in Babylon, Daniel observed Jeremiah's prophesy of seventy years (Jeremiah 25:12 and 29:10-11) for the completion of the desolations of Jerusalem. Daniel prayed, confessing his sin and the sin of the sons of Israel and asking God to have compassion and to restore Jerusalem and the temple:

> "O Lord, in accordance with all Your righteous acts, let now Your anger and Your wrath turn away from Your city Jerusalem…and for Your sake, O Lord, let Your face shine on Your desolate sanctuary."

Daniel 9:16-17
See Daniel 9:1-19

Even when threatened with the lions' den, Daniel continued to pray (Daniel 6:10), asking forgiveness, and God answered his prayer to restored Jerusalem and the temple. Ezekiel and Daniel were the two great prophets during the time of the deportation and exile.

About 150 years earlier, the Lord had spoken through the prophet Isaiah of a king (not yet born) of a kingdom (that did not yet exist):

> Thus says the LORD, your Redeemer… "It is I who says of Cyrus, 'He is My shepherd! And he will perform all My desire.'" And he declares of Jerusalem, "She will be built," and of the temple, "Your foundation will be laid".

Isaiah 44:24-28

Now in the first year of Cyrus, king of Persia, in order to fulfill the word of the Lord by the mouth of

Jeremiah, the Lord stirred up the spirit of Cyrus king of Persia so that he sent a proclamation throughout all his kingdom, and also put it in writing, saying, "Thus says Cyrus king of Persia, 'The LORD, the God of heaven, has given me all the kingdoms of the earth and He has appointed me to build Him a house in Jerusalem, which is in Judah'".

Ezra 1:1-2; 2 Chronicles 36:22-23

By the authority of this proclamation of Cyrus, as Isaiah had prophesied 150 years earlier and as Jeremiah had prophesied seventy years earlier, Zerubbabel led the first group of exiles from Babylon back to Judah to rebuild the temple. (Ezra 1-3). The promise went through Zerubbabel (Matthew 1:12-13). Through the prophet Haggai, God told Zerubbabel and the remnant of His people to finish rebuilding the temple (Haggai 1:1-11, Ezra 6:14). At that time, the prophet Haggai became the first, last, and only prophet the sons of Israel ever obeyed (Haggai 1:12-15, Ezra 5:1-2, Zechariah 1:1-6). They finished rebuilding the temple (Ezra 6:14-15) (remodeled later by Herod)[4] that Jesus Himself would walk in (Haggai 2:5, 9) about five hundred years later.

Ezra the priest led the second large return from exile (Ezra 7:1-10). The third return from Babylon to Judah was led by **Nehemiah** (Nehemiah 1-2), who rebuilt the wall around Jerusalem (Nehemiah 2:17 to 7:1).

In those days after the wall was completed, Ezra led a great revival (Nehemiah 8:6). As Ezra read from the book of the Law of Moses, the people stood from early morning to midday, listening attentively to God's Word (Nehemiah 8:1-8). I'm only guessing, but maybe Ezra read these words from the farewell address of Moses, the book of Deuteronomy, spoken almost a thousand years earlier:

> See, I am setting before you today a blessing and a curse: the blessing, if you listen to the commandments of the LORD your God, which I am commanding you today; and the curse, if you do not listen to the commandments of the LORD your God, but turn aside from the way which I am commanding you today...
>
> Deuteronomy 11:26-28

> So it shall be when all of these things have come upon you, the blessing and the curse which I have set before you, and you call them to mind in all nations where the LORD your God has banished you, and you return to the LORD your God and obey Him with all your heart and soul according to all that I command you today, you and your sons, then the LORD your God will restore you from captivity, and have compassion on you, and will gather you again from all the peoples where the LORD your God has scattered you.
>
> Deuteronomy 30:1-3

> I call heaven and earth to witness against you today, that I have set before you life and death, the blessing and the curse. So choose life in order that you

may live, you and your descendants, by loving the LORD your God, by obeying His voice, and by holding fast to Him; for this is your life and the length of your days, that you may *live in the land* which the LORD swore to your fathers, to Abraham, Isaac, and Jacob, to give them.

Deuteronomy 30:19-20 (italics mine)

All the people wept when they heard the words of the Law (Nehemiah 8:9).

Esther, the final historical book in the Old Testament, recounts God's protection of His people dispersed in the nations. The people of the Promise, referred to here as Jews,[5] are outside of God's will and plan for them, because they chose not to return and *live in the land* God had promised to give them (Jeremiah 29:10-20). Although neither God nor the name of God is mentioned in the book of Esther, still God protected these sons of Israel (Esther 8:3-11), who had lost faith in the *promise of God* and chose not to return and *live in the land*. Old Testament history ends with the book of Esther.

What are often called the poetic, or wisdom, books come next in the Old Testament: **Job, Psalms, Proverbs, Ecclesiastes**, and **Song of Solomon**. King David and King Solomon wrote much of this literature. The Psalms are songs that were sung by the people of God, often in the temple, beginning during the days of the kings. These songs expressing the emotions, fears, hopes, joys, praise, and worship of God's people remain a great encouragement today to

God's people. For many, the Psalms are a favorite portion of Scripture that is fittingly found right in the middle of the Bible. If you take your Bible in both hands and open it close to the middle, you will find the Psalms.

The Psalms also contain many references to the coming of Jesus.[6] These Psalms that refer to Jesus were written and sung about a thousand years before the birth of Jesus. Jesus Himself quoted some of them.

The Old Testament ends with the prophetic books: **Isaiah, Jeremiah, Lamentations, Ezekiel, Daniel, Hosea, Joel, Amos, Obadiah, Jonah, Micah, Nahum, Habakkuk, Zephaniah, Haggai, Zechariah** and **Malachi**. In his confession, Daniel prayed,

> We have not listened to Your servants the prophets, who spoke in Your name to our kings, our princes, our fathers and all the people of the land.
>
> Daniel 9:6; see 9:4-10

As Daniel expressed in his prayer, the prophets were God's servants who spoke the Word of God to the people of God. Most of the prophets lived during the times of the kings, but some lived and spoke after the return of God's people to the promised land from exile in Babylon. We have already quoted from some of the prophets, which are rich in references to the coming of Jesus.[7]

The prophet Malachi delivered a final message from God to His people, who did return to *live in the land* according to God's will (Ezkiel 36:22-28 and 37:21-28). Malachi's message and the Old Testament end with these words:

> Remember the law of Moses My servant, even the statutes and ordinances which I commanded him in Horeb for all Israel. Behold, I am going to send you Elijah the prophet before the coming of the great and terrible day of the LORD. He will restore the hearts of the fathers to their children and the hearts of the children to their fathers, so that I will not come and smite the land with a curse.

> Malachi 4:4-6

About 430 years of silence followed, in which no prophet spoke and the people of the promise, the children of Israel, did not hear the voice of their God. Then the final Old Testament prophet, John the Baptist (Matthew 11:9-14), appeared and proclaimed what all the prophets before him had longed to see (1 Peter 1:10-12).

> Behold, the Lamb of God who takes away the sin of the world!

> John 1:28-29

The promise of God made to Abraham that in him, all the families of the earth would be blessed (Genesis 12:3) was fulfilled in Jesus. (See Matthew 1:1-18.)

Behold His glory.
Behold, the Lamb of God who takes away the sin of the world.

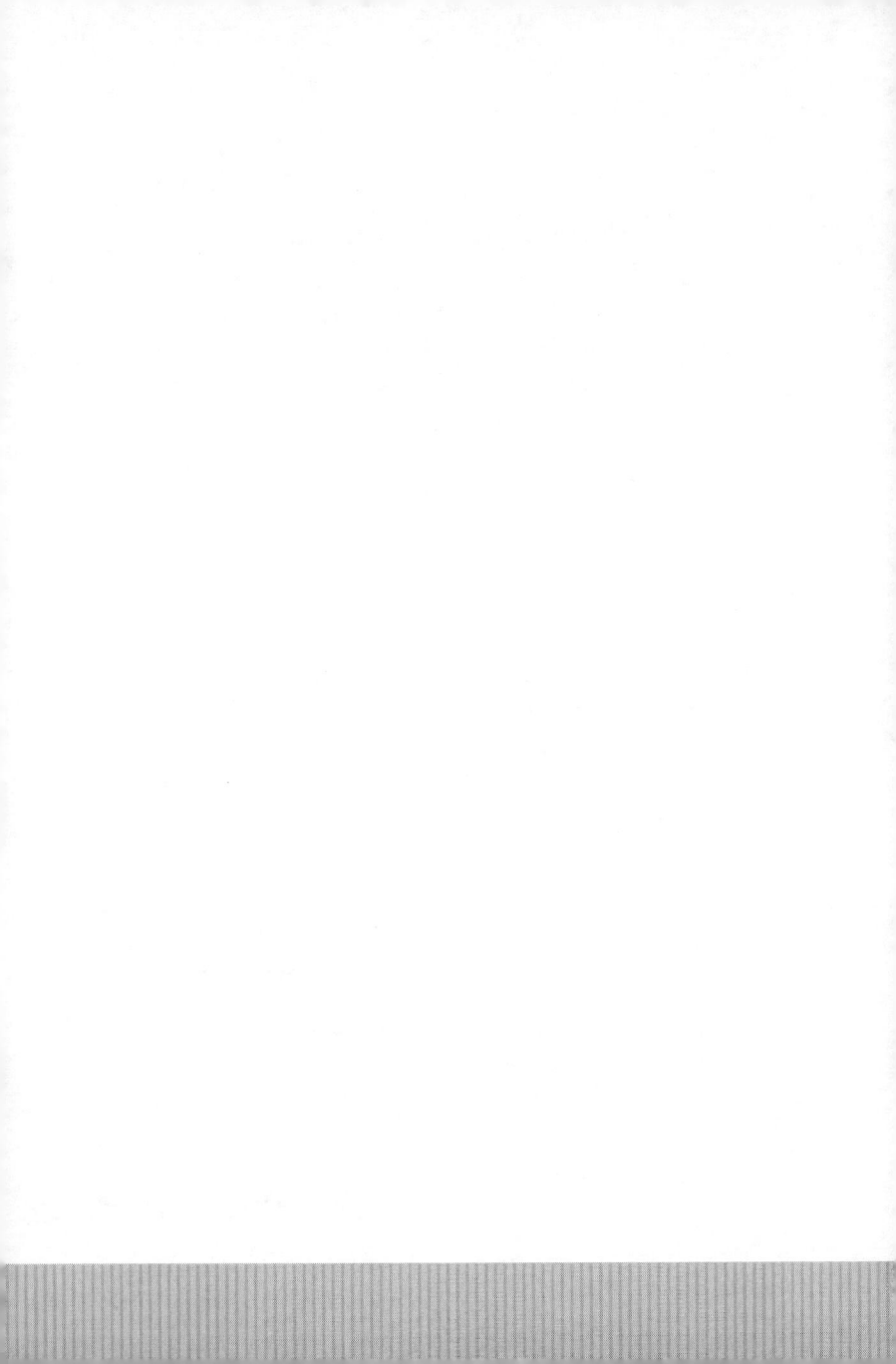

THE GOSPEL OF GOD

In the beginning God…

Then God said…and it was so.

Genesis 1:1, 6-7, 9, 11, 14-15, 24

These first words of the Bible, "In the beginning, God," are the foundation upon which the entire Bible stands or falls. If these words are not true, the Bible is nothing more than a hollow, empty sham, a myth or a fairy tale. But if these words are true, that is, if God is the source of everything we see and know, if all reality *begins* with and comes from the God of this book, then what you are about to read in the following pages is indeed good news from God, the gospel of God.

> Thus says the LORD, "Heaven is My throne and the earth is My footstool…For My hand made all these things, thus all these things came into being," declares the LORD.

> "But to this one I will look, to him who is humble and contrite of spirit, and who trembles at My *word*."

Isaiah 66:1-2 (italics mine)

In the beginning God…
created…
the heavens and the earth…
    Then God said…and it was so.

In the beginning was the *Word*
    Then God said…and it was so.

In the beginning was the *Word*
    God said…

and the *Word* was with God,
and the *Word* was God…
and the *Word* became flesh, and dwelt among us, and we beheld His glory, glory as of the only begotten from the Father, full of grace and truth… grace and truth were realized through Jesus Christ.

    Genesis 1:1, 6-7; John 1:1, 14, 17 (italics mine)

Now the birth of Jesus Christ was as follows. When His mother Mary had been betrothed to Joseph, before they came together, she was found to be with child by the Holy Spirit. And Joseph, her husband, being a righteous man and not wanting to disgrace her, planned to send her away secretly. But when he had considered this, behold, an angel of the Lord appeared to him in a dream, saying, "Joseph, son of David, do not be afraid to take Mary as your wife; for the Child who has been conceived in her is of the Holy Spirit. She will bear a Son; and you shall call His name *Savior*, for He will *save*…

- In Hebrew/Aramaic, the language in which the angel spoke these words to Joseph – יֵשׁוּעַ, Yeshua.

- In Greek, the language in which these words were first written down – Ἰησοῦς, Iesous.

- In English, the language in which you are reading these words – Jesus.

- In meaning – Savior.[8]

> "She will bear a Son; and you shall call His name *Savior*, for He will *save* His people from their sins." Now all this took place to fulfill what was spoken by the Lord through the prophet: "'Behold, the virgin shall be with child and shall bear a son, and they shall call his name Immanuel,' which translated means, 'God with us.'" And Joseph awoke from his sleep and did as the angel of the Lord commanded him and took Mary as his wife but kept her a virgin until she gave birth to a Son, and he called His name *Savior*.

> Matthew 1.18-25 (italics mine; to give the flavor of what Joseph actually heard the angel say, יֵשׁוּעַ, I have chosen to translate rather than transliterate in the above passage with my apology to the Lockman Foundation.)

Even though it is not scriptural, I sometimes imagine a group of children gathered at the door of a house in Nazareth calling out, "Mary, Mary, can *Savior* come out and play?" That was His name, given to Him at birth by Joseph, as the angel commanded. That is what people called Him His whole life, *Savior*.

Now, in those days a decree went out from Caesar Augustus that a census be taken of all the inhabited earth. This was the first census taken while Quirinius was governor of Syria. And everyone was on his way to register for the census, each to his own city. Joseph also went up from Galilee, from the city of Nazareth, to Judea, to the city of David, which is called Bethlehem, because he was of the house and family of David, in order to register along with Mary, who was engaged to him and was with child.

While they were there, the days were completed for her to give birth. And she gave birth to her firstborn son, and she wrapped Him in cloths and laid Him in a manger because there was no room for them in the inn.

In the same region, there were some shepherds staying out in the fields and keeping watch over their flock by night. And an angel of the Lord suddenly stood before them, and the glory of the Lord shone around them, and they were terribly frightened. But the angel said to them, "Do not be afraid; for behold, I bring you *gospel*…[9]

Throughout the entire New Testament, this root is often rendered *gospel*, but not always. For example, right here, the translators have chosen to render it "good news," which is, of course, the meaning of the word *gospel*.

But the angel said to them, "Do not be afraid; for behold, I bring you *gospel*…good news…of great joy which will be for all the people."

And what is this gospel which is for everyone? What is this gospel message intended to bring great joy to all people? Here it is, the gospel:

> For today in the city of David, there has been born for you a Savior, who is Christ the Lord.

That's it. That is the gospel, the good news that God Himself proclaimed from heaven by an angel the night Jesus was born: "A Savior who is Christ the Lord is born for you."

> This will be a sign for you: you will find a baby wrapped in cloths and lying in a manger." And suddenly, there appeared with the angel a multitude of the heavenly host praising God and saying, "Glory to God in the highest, And on earth peace…good will toward men.

"In the highest" heaven, the result of the proclamation of the gospel on earth is praise that brings "glory to God." On earth, the result of the proclamation of the gospel is "peace." The gospel, the good news, expresses God's "good will toward men," and the intent of God's "good will toward men" is "peace," that is, the reconciliation of men with God. Because a Savior who is Christ the Lord is born for you, there is "Glory to God in the highest (heaven), and on earth (there can be) peace, (reconciliation between God and man because of God's) good will toward men."

> When the angels had gone away from them into heaven, the shepherds began saying to one another, "Let us go straight to Bethlehem then and see this thing that has happened which the Lord has made known to us." So they came in a hurry and found their way to Mary and Joseph and the baby as He lay in the manger. When they had seen this, they made known the statement that had been told them about this Child. (*"A Savior who is Christ the Lord is born for you."*)
>
> And all who heard it wondered at the things that were told them by the shepherds. (*"A Savior who is Christ the Lord is born for you."*)
>
> But Mary treasured all these things, pondering them in her heart. (*"A Savior who is Christ the Lord is born for me."*)
>
> The shepherds went back, glorifying and praising God for all that they had heard and seen, just as had been told them. (*"A Savior who is Christ the Lord is born for you."*)
>
> Luke 2:1-20
> (Comments in italics and the alternate
> translation of εὐαγγελίζομαι are mine.)

"Now after John had been taken into custody, Jesus came into Galilee, preaching the *gospel of God...*" Jesus was preaching, I believe, the gospel that God Himself proclaimed from heaven the night Jesus was born: "A Savior who is Christ the Lord is born for you."

> Now after John had been taken into custody, Jesus came into Galilee, preaching the *gospel of God (preaching that "A Savior who is Christ the Lord is born for you")* and saying, "The time is fulfilled, and the kingdom of God is at hand; repent and believe in the gospel." (*Repent and believe that a Savior who is Christ the Lord is born for you*).
>
> As He was going along by the Sea of Galilee, He saw Simon and Andrew, the brother of Simon, casting a net in the sea; for they were fishermen. And Jesus said to them, "(*A Savior who is Christ the Lord is born for you.*) Follow Me, and I will make you become…".
>
> Mark 1:14-17 (Comments in italics are mine.)

A Savior who is Christ the Lord is born for you, Simon. "Follow Me, and I will make you become…"

Andrew, a Savior who is Christ the Lord is born for you. "Follow Me, and I will make you become…"

If you follow Me, I'll change your life…I'll change you…

Starting wherever you are at this moment, if you follow Me, "I will make you become" something new, the kind of person that draws men and women to Me, "fishers of men" (Mark 1:14-17).

From eternity past the heart of the Christmas story is *the Gospel of God*, the gospel that God Himself proclaimed from heaven the night Jesus was born. This is the same gospel I believe Jesus preached with a personal invitation: "A Savior who is Christ the Lord is born for you. Follow Me, and I will make you become…"

After the death and resurrection of Jesus, the Apostle Paul summarized the gospel as follows.

> Now I make known to you, brethren, *the gospel*…that *Christ died for our sins* according to the Scriptures, and that *He was buried*, and that *He was raised on the third day* according to the Scriptures, and that *He appeared*…"
>
> 1 Corinthians 15:1-5 (italics mine)

This is the *Gospel of God*, the good news, proclaimed in Scripture:

> A Savior who is Christ the Lord is born for you.
> He died for our sins.
> He was buried.
> He was raised on the third day.
> He appeared.

Behold His glory.

THE SON OF GOD

Who is the man?

John 5:12

I stood looking into a deep hole in the ground on the north side of Mount Moriah, the temple mount in Jerusalem. If you go to the pool of Bethesda today, that's all that is left, just a pile of rocks and ruble around two holes in the ground. While our guide made his remarks, I admit that I wasn't listening very well.

We were given a few minutes to relax or to explore, so I took a slow walk alone along the path around the rubble of what used to be the five porches and the upper and lower pools of Bethesda. Standing alone, I remembered what happened there and the words of Jesus that have become part of the foundation of everything I believe and who I am today. Remember?

> Now there is in Jerusalem by the sheep gate a pool, which is called in Hebrew Bethesda, having five porticoes. In these lay a multitude of those who were sick, blind, lame, and withered. A man was

there who had been ill for thirty-eight years. When Jesus saw him lying there, and knew that he had already been a long time in that condition, He said to him, "Do you wish to get well?"

John 5:2-6

This man was a man of tremendous faith. His faith was the focus of all his thoughts and the dominating force in his life. There was no one who knew him who did not also know what he believed. This man believed in the healing power of the pool of Bethesda to the extent that his faith controlled every waking moment of his life. His entire life was a public testimony to his great faith in the healing power of the pool of Bethesda and his hope to someday be healed in it. I wish I could say that about my faith, that it controls my life to such an extent that everyone who knows me knows what I believe. That is the kind of tremendous faith this man had.

"A man was there who had been ill for thirty-eight years." Think of it. This man of tremendous faith had been sick for thirty-eight years. So if his faith was so great, where was God during all that time?

When Jesus saw him lying there and knew that he had already been a long time in that condition, He said to him, "Do you wish to get well?"

John 5:6

The man had been sick for thirty-eight years, and Jesus asked him, "Do you wish to get well?" What was Jesus thinking?

Listen to the man's answer:

> Sir, I have no man to put me into the pool when the water is stirred up, but while I am coming, another steps down before me"
>
> John 5:7

Poor me. "I have no man to put me into the pool." No one will help me. No one cares about me. Everyone takes advantage of me. "While I am coming, another steps down before me." This guy is having a regular pity party.

The sick man's answer tells us something more about him. As he spoke to Jesus, it is obvious that the sick man did not realize he was speaking to the all-powerful, life-giving, eternal God worthy of his worship. The sick man's great faith was not in Jesus but in the healing power of the pool of Bethesda. His plea was only for the attention and sympathy of Jesus, and a little help getting into the pool.

As a boy, I lived far enough north that ponds and lakes sometimes froze over hard. I once saw the ice on a lake frozen thick enough that the lake looked something like a parking lot with cars and pickup trucks parked all over it beside holes men had chipped in the ice to fish in.

An interesting thing about ice is that you cannot always tell just by looking at it how thick it is. Ice freezes from the bottom surface of the ice down, that is, thickness is added to the bottom surface of the ice as it freezes. Ice also melts from the bottom surface up. That means that the appearance of the top surface of the ice can remain relatively unchanged. Especially with a dusting of fresh snow, by just looking at ice, you cannot always tell whether it is dangerously thin or thick enough to safely drive a car on. I know. After stepping through thin ice once, I became very aware of the danger of thin ice.

Let me ask you a question. Who do you think is more secure? Is the person with tremendous faith who steps out without hesitation and without doubt onto dangerously thin ice more secure? Or is the one with doubt and very little faith who hesitatingly and fearfully steps out onto ice thick enough to safely support a car more secure?

I'll tell you what. You can have the strong faith. I'll take the strong ice every time. You see, your security does not depend on how much faith you have. Your security depends on the object of your faith. Strong faith placed in something uncertain is insecure at best and quite possibly dangerous. However, only a very little faith, say, the size of a mustard seed, just enough faith to step out on what is certain and true results in complete security. Your security does not depend on the strength of your faith but rather on the strength of the object of your faith, that is, on the certainty of what you believe in.

When Jesus asked him, "Do you wish to get well?" Jesus saw the man's heart and knew what he believed in. As Jesus listened to his expression of faith in the pool and his plea, I'm sure Jesus knew that He was about to ask the man to make a decision that would change his entire life. Jesus was about to ask the man to change the object of his faith from the healing power of the pool of Bethesda to the healing power of God the Son.

> Jesus said to him, "Get up, pick up your pallet and walk."
>
> John 5:8

I wonder if their eyes met when Jesus spoke. I know that Jesus got his attention because the focus of this man's faith became Jesus and His Word. The man changed the object of his faith from the pool of Bethesda to Jesus, God the Son. How do I know? Because he placed his hope in Jesus, he responded to the Word of Jesus and he obeyed. Jesus said, "Get up," and "immediately the man became well." Jesus said, "Pick up your pallet," and he "picked up his pallet." Jesus said, "Walk," and he "began to walk."

Jesus applied His Word to this man. Jesus, the very same God who said, "Let there be light," and there was light (Genesis 1:3; 2 Corinthians 4:6), now said with the same authority, "Get up, pick up your pallet and walk." The Word of God, Scripture, applied to his life, to your life, and to my life, is powerful when we hear it, believe it, and obey it.

> Immediately the man became well, and picked up his pallet and began to walk.
>
> Now it was the Sabbath on that day. So the Jews were saying to the man who was cured, "It is the

Sabbath, and it is not permissible for you to carry your pallet."

But he answered them, "He who made me well was the one who said to me, 'Pick up your pallet and walk.'"

They asked him, "*Who is the man* who said to you, 'Pick up your pallet and walk'?"

John 5:9-12 (italics mine)

At this point the Jews ask the question of the hour: *"Who is the man?"* We finally get to the central issue here and the main point of the entire passage: who is this guy? Who is Jesus? If the man who had just been healed thought his sickness and the pool of Bethesda were the central issues in his life, he was wrong. If you think the central issue in your life is something else, you are wrong too. The central issue in this man's life, in your life, and in my life is one and the same: *"Who is the man?"* Who is Jesus to you?

But the man who was healed did not know who it was, for Jesus had slipped away while there was a crowd in that place. Afterward Jesus found him in the temple.

John 5:13-14

That says a lot about the man. After Jesus healed him, where was he? He was in the temple. Do you suppose that after being healed, he might have started looking for God?

For "a long time," maybe for as long as thirty-eight years, he had been looking with great faith for help in the wrong place, at the pool of Bethesda, and not finding it. But now in the temple, God the Son found him. Let me ask you a question. Where are you looking for help? Where do you want to find help, in your own benefit; in your own welfare; or in God Himself, in His Word, in His works, and in His will for you? You see, what the sick man sought was healing. But what God the Son sought was him. I don't know what you want right now. But I know what Jesus wants. Jesus wants you. Jesus wants you to know Him and the power of His resurrection.

> Afterward Jesus found him in the temple and said to him, "Behold, you have become well; do not sin anymore, so that nothing worse happens to you."
>
> John 5:14.

The man had been sick for thirty-eight years. That might be longer than you have been alive. For most of us, thirty-eight years would be at least the majority of our life, if not all or almost all of it. Can you imagine being sick for thirty-eight years? Can you think of anything worse that could happen to you than lying flat on your back, sick, for all or most of your life? What could be worse than that? Jesus said that the consequences of sin are worse. And who would know any better than Jesus, who faced the cross? Listen carefully to the Word of Jesus:

"Behold, you have become well; do not sin anymore, so that nothing worse happens to you."

The man went away, and told the Jews that it was Jesus who had made him well. For that reason the Jews were persecuting Jesus, because He was doing those things on the Sabbath. But He answered them, "My Father is working until now, and I Myself am working." For this reason therefore the Jews were seeking all the more to kill Him, because He not only was breaking the Sabbath, but also was calling God His own Father, making Himself equal with God.

John 5:15-18

There is the accusation. Jesus did not refer to God as *our* Father who art in heaven. Jesus called God "*My* Father." Jesus "was calling God His own Father," like He had some kind of special relationship with God. But worse, Jesus was comparing Himself with God, "making Himself equal with God."

To understand this accusation, you need to hear the words of Jesus like the Jews heard them. Not our father, Jesus said,

"My Father is working until now, and I Myself am working."

That is, My Father is working…and I am working. God is working…and I am working. And the Jews said, "Wait a minute. Hold it! Jesus is comparing His work to God's work in the same sentence. Blasphemy! Who does He think He is, equal with God?"

> "For this reason therefore the Jews were seeking all the more to kill Him, because He…was calling God His own Father, making Himself equal with God."

Remember the Jews' question, "Who is the man?" Who is this guy? Who is Jesus? On the table right here might be the most important question in the Bible. You have heard the accusation that Jesus was "making Himself equal with God." How do you think Jesus responded to this charge? Do you think Jesus replied, "No, no! That's not what I meant. This is all just a misunderstanding. Calm down. Let me explain"? Is that what Jesus said? No, not at all. Listen carefully to His answer. Listen to what Jesus claimed about Himself in His response to the accusation that He was "making Himself equal with God." If this is the most important question in the Bible, "Who is the man?" "Who is Jesus?" then you are about to hear Jesus give the most important answer in the Bible.

"Therefore *Jesus answered*…" This is the answer Jesus gave to the accusation that He was comparing Himself with God, that He was "making Himself equal with God."

> Therefore Jesus answered and was saying to them, "Truly, truly, I say to you, the Son can do nothing of Himself, unless it is something He sees the Father doing; for whatever the Father does, these things the Son also does *in like manner*."
>
> John 5:19 (italics mine)

What does God do? God the Father does whatever He wills without restraint because He is all-powerful. "For whatever the Father does, these things the Son also does in like manner." "*In like manner*"—Jesus is comparing Himself with God. Jesus claimed to do whatever God does "in like manner"; that is, Jesus claimed to be equal in power and authority with God. The claim of Jesus is clear: I am as powerful as God. Whatever God does, I do "in like manner."

> For the Father loves the Son, and shows Him all things that He Himself is doing; and the Father will show Him greater works than these, so that you will marvel. For *just as* the Father raises the dead and gives them life, *even so* the Son also gives life to whom He wishes.
>
> John 5:20-21(italics mine)

God created life, and only God can give life. Jesus said, "*even so*," that is, "*just as*" only God can do, I give life.

"You accuse me of comparing myself with God, of making myself equal with God," Jesus said. "Let Me explain this as clearly as I can. Whatever God does, I do '*in like manner*.' I am as powerful as God. *Just as* only God can give life. *Even so*, that is, 'in the same way' as only God can do, I give life."

> "For not even the Father judges anyone, but He has given all judgment to the Son, so that all will honor the Son *even as* they honor the Father. He who does not honor the Son does not honor the Father who sent Him."
>
> John 5:22-23 (italics mine)

It is the Father's purpose "that all will honor the Son *even as* they honor the Father…" "*Even as*"—there Jesus goes again comparing Himself with God. Jesus said that the Son is to be honored "*even as*"; that is, "in the same way" the Father is honored. Jesus is claiming that He is worthy to be honored and worshipped "*even as*" God.

There may have been some Jews present who were a little slow to pick up on what Jesus was saying and where He was taking all of this. I can guarantee you that if not before, by this point Jesus had their attention. This is a serious claim. When Jesus claims He is worthy to be honored and worshipped "*even as*" God, either Jesus is God, or this is pure blasphemy. But Jesus does not leave this point with only a comparison between Himself and God. Jesus goes on to say,

> "He who does not honor the Son does not honor the Father who sent Him."

"If you don't honor and worship Me," Jesus said, "you're not worshiping God, because I am your God."

> Truly, truly, I say to you, he who hears My word, and believes Him who sent Me, has eternal life, and does not come into judgment, but has passed out of death into life. Truly, truly, I say to you, an hour is coming and now is, when the dead will hear the voice of the Son of God, and those who hear will live. For *just as* the Father has life in Himself, *even so* He gave to the Son also to have life in Himself."

> John 5:24-26 (italics mine)

Only God has not received life from another source, because God "has life in Himself." Only God is eternal. And again, Jesus compares Himself with God: "*Even so* He gave to the Son also to have life in Himself." Neither did Jesus receive life, because Jesus has "life in Himself." Only God is eternal, and Jesus claimed to be eternal.

The enemies of Jesus accused Jesus of comparing Himself with God, of "making Himself equal with God." If you have any doubt about who Jesus claimed to be, consider carefully the response of Jesus to their accusation:

> Only God is all-powerful. Jesus claimed to be all-powerful.
>
> Only God can give life. Jesus claimed to give life.
>
> Only God is worthy of our worship. Jesus claimed to be worthy of honor and worship "*even as*" God.
>
> Only God is eternal. Jesus claimed to be eternal.

Either these words of Jesus are the words of God Himself, God the Son as He claimed to be, or Jesus is the most wicked, evil, perverted, damned liar who ever lived. One thing is certain. Jesus is not just a good man, a good teacher, or a prophet. A good man does not walk around claiming to be God.

If you are not sure who Jesus is, I challenge you to read the Gospel of John in the Bible from beginning to end, concentrating on all of the words of Jesus. (Some Bibles highlight the words of Jesus in red.) You decide. Are these the words of a wicked, evil, perverted liar? Some have suggested that Jesus was self-deceived, that is, crazy. He just thought He was God, but He really wasn't. Read His own words in the Gospel of John and judge for yourself. Are the words of Jesus the words of a liar or a lunatic? Or is the *word* of Jesus the truth, and is Jesus the One He claims to be, the almighty, life-giving, eternal God worthy of our worship?[10]

In the midst of what Jesus claimed about Himself, did you catch His invitation?

> "Truly, truly, I say to you, he who hears My *word*, and believes Him who sent Me, has eternal life, and does not come into judgment, but has passed out of death into life."
>
> John 5:24 (italics mine)

This offer from Jesus of eternal life is for anyone who will hear His word and believe that His word is the word of God, "Him who sent Me." Jesus said, "When you hear 'My word,' you are hearing the word of your God, of God Himself, the one who sent me." Do you believe that? Jesus said, "He who hears My word, and believes…has eternal life."

"*Who is the man?*" Who is Jesus? The sick man's problem was not a lack of faith. The sick man's problem was the object of his faith. He did not know who was speaking to him. He did not know Jesus. Jesus did not challenge him to have more faith, to increase the fervency of his faith. Jesus challenged the sick man to change the object of his faith, to change what he believed in.

The central issue in this man's life, in your life, in my life, and in all of life was stated clearly by the Jews. "*Who is the man?*" Who is Jesus? The Jews then accused Jesus of comparing Himself with God, of making Himself out to be equal with God. In response to their accusation, Jesus claimed to be the almighty, life-giving, eternal God worthy of our worship. Do you hear His claim? Do you believe the *word* of Jesus? When the sick man heard the word of Jesus and believed, God the Son changed his life. If you hear the *word* of Jesus and believe, Jesus will change your life.

> "Truly, truly, I say to you, he who hears My *word*, and believes…has eternal life."
>
> John 5:24 (italics mine)

An hour is coming and already is when those who hear the voice of the Son of God shall live.

Behold His glory.

THE WORKS OF GOD

As He passed by, He saw a man blind from birth. And His disciples asked Him, "Rabbi, who sinned, this man or his parents, that he would be born blind?"

Jesus answered, "It was neither that this man sinned, nor his parents; but it was so that *the works of God* might be displayed in him."

John 9:1-3 (italics mine)

Years ago in Jalisco, Mexico, a lady named Irma asked me to lead an evangelistic Bible study in her apartment because she wanted to tell her friends and neighbors about Jesus. The first evening, it was just Irma and two of her adult children present, but as the weeks passed, the group grew in number until her living room was beyond capacity.

One evening after the Bible study, Irma asked me to stay a moment. She began to tell me her life story. As a mother of three children, Irma discovered her husband had a *casa chica*, which is to say he was married to a second woman and supported both wives and families. Because he traveled a lot, neither wife was aware of the other.

Irma described how her children had been affected by the divorce. At the end of her story, Irma explained that she had forgiven her husband for what he did to her, but then she added through tears, "*No puedo perdonarle por lo que el me hizo a los hijos. ¿Qué hago?*" That is, "I cannot forgive him for what he did to my children. What do I do?" Then came the hard question: "*¿Cómo permite Dios que ese hombre les cause tanto sufrimiento a mis hijos?*" "How could God allow that man to cause so much suffering for my children?"

I had no answer. But when we came to chapter 9 in our study of the Gospel of John several weeks later, I marveled at God's response to Irma's question about suffering. While I have shared the following with others over the years, it will always remain for me what it was that first time I shared it in Spanish: God's personal response to the cry of Irma's heart.

When Jesus saw this blind man, His disciples asked Him about suffering. Why was this man born blind? Is he suffering for his own sins, or the sins of his parents? "Rabbi, who sinned, this man or his parents, that he would be born blind?"

Why do you think the disciples of Jesus phrased their question about suffering like this? I believe it was because they had heard and understood the teaching of the Scriptures. This is, in fact, what the Old Testament teaches, that suffering is a consequence of sin. I must hasten to add that this is not the whole counsel of God about suffering. Jesus has something very important to say to His disciples and to us about suffering in this passage. But to hear the words of Jesus as the disciples heard them, in the context of Old Testament Scripture, we might first need a little review of what the disciples seemed to already know by heart.

The prophet Jeremiah described the destruction of Jerusalem by the Babylonians with these words:

> "Her adversaries have become her masters, her enemies prosper; for the LORD has caused her grief because of the multitude of her transgressions."
>
> Lamentations 1:5

The Lord caused the grief of His people because of the multitude of their transgressions. It was no accident. They suffered because of their sins.

After Nehemiah's return and his successful reconstruction of the wall around Jerusalem, the prophet Ezra led a great revival in Jerusalem. As in all revivals, central to this revival was confession and a re-focus on the Lord and His Word. Listen to the words of Nehemiah's confession to God:

> But they became disobedient and rebelled against You, and cast Your law behind their backs and killed Your prophets who had admonished them so that they might return to You, and they committed great blasphemies. Therefore You delivered them into the hand of their oppressors who oppressed them…
>
> Nehemiah 9:26-27

It was God who delivered His people into the hand of their oppressors. Why? They suffered because they "became disobedient" to God. They suffered because they "rebelled against" God. They suffered because they turned their back on God's Word and those who proclaimed God's Word. Disobedient, rebellious, turned away from God's Word and God's messengers, they committed great blasphemies, great sins. So God delivered them into the hand of their oppressors to suffer for their sins.

Moses gave this penetrating admonition:

> "But if you will not do so, behold, you have sinned against the LORD, and be sure your sin will find you out."

> Numbers 32:23

"Be sure your sin will find you out". It is the clear teaching of Scripture that sin has consequences both allowed and caused (Lamentations 1:5) by God for the good of His people, that we may share His holiness and be conformed to the image and to the glory of His Son, Jesus (Isaiah 42:23-25; Hebrews 12:9-10, 12:1-11; Galatians 6:7-8; Romans 15:4 and 8:28-30). This message echoes throughout the Old Testament: my sin will result in my suffering. Ezekiel put it bluntly: "The soul who sins will die" (Ezekiel 18:4). And so the disciples asked Jesus, "Was this man born blind because of his own sin?"

The entire book of Numbers details one of the great Old Testament examples of suffering for sin. Numbers is the story of the wandering of the sons of Israel in the wilderness for forty years because they refused to believe the promise of God that He would bring them safely into the land He had promised to give them. Listen to God's words about suffering:

> Surely you shall not come into the land in which I swore to settle you, except Caleb the son of Jephunneh and Joshua the son of Nun. Your children, however, whom you said would become a prey—I will bring them in, and they will know the land which you have rejected. But as for you, your corpses will fall in this wilderness. Your sons shall be shepherds for forty years in the wilderness, and they will suffer for your unfaithfulness, until your corpses lie in the wilderness.

> Numbers 14:30-33

Who sinned? The parents sinned. They rejected the promise of God. And who suffered? The parents suffered. Except for Caleb and Joshua, all those twenty years of age or older at Kadesh-barnea wandered in the wilderness until they died. Because of their sin, they never entered the promised land.

Did you notice who else suffered? The children suffered for the sin of their parents: "Your children...your sons...will suffer for your unfaithfulness."

Both the parents and their children suffered for the sin of the parents. It is the clear teaching of scripture that we not only suffer for our own sins. We also suffer for the sins of those around us, who, in turn, suffer with us for our sins.

In the book of Numbers, the children suffered for the sins of their parents. We could multiply examples of children today who suffer for the sins of their parents, and vice versa, I might add. How many parents suffer because of the sins of their children?

The book of Joshua contains another clear example of suffering for the sins of those around us:

> But the sons of Israel acted unfaithfully in regard to the things under the ban, for Achan, the son of Carmi, the son of Zabdi, the son of Zerah, from the tribe of Judah, took some of the things under the ban; therefore, the anger of the LORD burned against the sons of Israel. Now Joshua sent men from Jericho to Ai, which is near Beth-aven, east of Bethel, and said to them, "Go up and spy out the land." So the men went up and spied out Ai. They returned to Joshua and said to him, "Do not let all the people go up; only about two or three thousand men need go up to Ai; do not make all the people toil up there, for they are few." So about three thousand men from the people went up there, but they fled from the men of Ai. The men of Ai struck down about thirty-six of their men, and pursued them from the gate as far as Shebarim and struck them down on the descent, so the hearts of the people melted and became as water.
>
> Joshua 7:1-5

Because of the sin of one man, Achan, "the anger of the LORD burned against the sons of Israel." Who sinned? Achan. And who suffered? To be sure, Achan suffered:

> So Achan answered Joshua and said, "Truly, I have sinned against the LORD, the God of Israel…" Then Joshua and all Israel with him, took Achan the son of Zerah, the silver, the mantle, the bar of gold, his sons, his daughters, his oxen, his donkeys, his sheep, his tent and all that belonged to him; and they brought them up to the valley of Achor. Joshua said, "Why have you troubled us? The LORD will trouble you this day." And all Israel stoned them with stones; and they burned them with fire after they had stoned them with stones.

Joseph 7:20 and 24-25

Achan was stoned to death for his own sin, but not only Achan suffered for his sin. His sons and his daughters were also stoned with him. But the consequences of Achan's sin reached even beyond his own family. Remember?

"The anger of the LORD burned against the sons of Israel."

Joshua asked, "Why have you troubled *us*?" Remember, the men of Ai struck down about thirty-six men of Israel. In addition to Achan and his family, about thirty-six men died in the battle that day because of the sin of Achan. These men and their families also suffered because of Achan's sin.

While we were missionaries, we were robbed twice and assaulted on another occasion. When we came home after being robbed and found the house ransacked and our possessions thrown everywhere, we felt violated and in personal danger even though the thief found little that interested him. He took everything electronic we had, which consisted of a small, portable radio/cassette player that we called a boom box in those days. He also took a camera and lenses, one of my prize possessions. And finally, he took my wife's high school class ring.

Who sinned? The thief, of course. And who suffered? Scripture teaches that the thief suffered for his sin. But we also suffered because of the thief's sin? We replaced the boom box so that the music did not go out of our children's lives, but we lost the ability to document our work and family memories with photos, and my wife's class ring was irreplaceable. We suffered with the thief because of his sin.

Here's another example. If I am provoked to unrighteous anger, who suffers? Those around me, often my family, suffer my sinful outburst. The teaching of Scripture is clear. Not only do we suffer for our own sins. We also suffer for the sins of those around us, who, in turn, suffer with us for ours.

The same is true on an even larger scale. Political leaders are the ones who declare wars. And who suffers? Sometimes the politicians get caught, but most of the suffering and dying in war is done by others, by our sons on the battlefield. Common people often suffer for the arrogance and sin of their leaders.

An understanding of the consequences of sin does not begin to be complete without a look at the first sin:

Now the serpent was more crafty than any beast of the field which the Lord God had made. And he said to the woman, "Indeed, has God said, 'You shall not eat from any tree of the garden'?"

The woman said to the serpent, "From the fruit of the trees of the garden we may eat; but from the fruit of the tree which is in the middle of the garden, God has said, 'You shall not eat from it or touch it, or you will die.'"

The serpent said to the woman, "You surely will not die! For God knows that in the day you eat from it your eyes will be opened, and you will be like God, knowing good and evil."

When the woman saw that the tree was good for food, and that it was a delight to the eyes, and that the tree was desirable to make one wise, she took from its fruit and ate; and she gave also to her husband with her, and he ate. Then the eyes of both of them were opened, and they knew that they were naked; and they sewed fig leaves together and made themselves loin coverings.

They heard the sound of the Lord God walking in the garden in the cool of the day, and the man and his wife hid themselves from the presence of the Lord God among the trees of the garden. Then the Lord God called to the man, and said to him, "Where are you?"

He said, "I heard the sound of You in the garden, and I was afraid because I was naked; so I hid myself."

Genesis 3:1-10

This account of how Satan tempted Adam and Eve in the garden of Eden reminds us of the very first sin, Satan's sin, which caused his own fall. In arrogant blasphemy, Satan boasted: "I will ascend above the heights of the clouds; I will make myself *like the Most High*." (Isaiah 14:14; italics mine). At the heart of Satan's lie to Eve is this same temptation: "Your eyes will be opened, and *you will be like God*, knowing good and evil."

You can make yourself like the Most High, knowing good and evil. Don't you want to be like God? Don't you want to know both good and evil?

Sound tempting? But remember God's design for us: "God saw all that He had made, and behold, it was very good" (Genesis 1:31).

God's creation, His design for us, was all good. All that He had made was very good. It was God's intent that we know and experience only good, not good and evil.

Evil only entered as a consequence of sin, not by God's design, which was all good. After their sin, that evil was first manifested in the relationship of the man and the woman with each other. Before their sin, "the man and his wife were both naked and were not ashamed" (Genesis 2:25). But after they ate, "Then the eyes of both of them were opened, and they knew that they were naked; and they sewed fig leaves together and made themselves loin coverings." (Genesis 3:7)

Separation is always a consequence of sin. Sin always creates barriers between people. After their sin, Adam and Eve were ashamed, so they made themselves coverings. The first consequence of human sin mentioned in Scripture is a separation between the man and his wife. Their sin created a barrier, a separation in their relationship. Because of sin, they were ashamed, so they hid from each other.

Suppose I slander you, or lie to you, or lie about you, or commit any other sin against you. What effect will my sin have on our relationship with each other? Sin never builds relationships. Sin only creates barriers between people. Whatever the sin, it always causes some degree of separation between people.

The first sin not only caused a separation between these two people; it also separated them from their God.

"They heard the sound of the LORD God walking in the garden in the cool of the day, and the man and his wife hid themselves from the presence of the LORD God among the trees of the garden" (Genesis 3:8).

Because of sin, the man and his wife were separated from God. They not only hid from each other; they hid themselves from the presence of the Lord God.

When God called to the man, "Where are you?" He wasn't saying, "Adam! Oh, Adam! I can't find you." God knew exactly where He was and where Adam was. I believe God was saying to the man, "We used to walk together. Do you see what your sin has done to our relationship? Just look at yourself. Where are you, Adam? Hiding from me. You are separated from Me and afraid because of your sin." Sin not only separates us from each other, sin separates us from God.

> "Behold, the Lord's hand is not so short that it cannot save; nor is His ear so dull that it cannot hear. But your iniquities have made a separation between you and your God…"

> Isaiah 59:1-2

While separation is the first consequence of sin mentioned in Scripture, sin has another terrible consequence:

> And He said, "Who told you that you were naked? Have you eaten from the tree of which I commanded you not to eat?"

> The man said, "The woman whom You gave to be with me, she gave me from the tree, and I ate."

> Then the Lord God said to the woman, "What is this you have done?"

> And the woman said, "The serpent deceived me, and I ate."

> The Lord God said to the serpent, "Because you have done this, cursed are you more than all cattle, and more than every beast of the field; on your

belly you will go, and dust you will eat all the days of your life; and I will put enmity between you and the woman, and between your seed and her seed; he shall bruise you on the head, and you shall bruise him on the heel."

To the woman He said, "I will greatly multiply your pain in childbirth, in pain you will bring forth children; yet your desire will be for your husband, and he will rule over you."

Then to Adam He said, "Because you have listened to the voice of your wife, and have eaten from the tree about which I commanded you, saying, "You shall not eat from it', cursed is the ground because of you. In toil you will eat of it all the days of your life. Both thorns and thistles it shall grow for you, and you will eat the plants of the field. By the sweat of your face you will eat bread, till you return to the ground, because from it you were taken, for you are dust, and to dust you shall return."

Genesis 3:11-19

Along with separation, the other terrible consequence of sin is suffering. Take a look at who sinned and the consequences of each sin.

First, the serpent sinned. His sin was deceit, a lie.

The serpent deceived…

And who suffered for this sin? The serpent.

Because you have done this, cursed are you…

But did you see who else suffered for the sin of the serpent?

> Because you have done this, cursed are you more
> than all cattle, and more than every beast of the field.

While the serpent was cursed more, all the cattle and all the beasts of the field were cursed with him. It was not only the serpent that suffered for his sin. All the cattle and all the beasts of the field also suffer the curse of the serpent's sin.

Next, the woman sinned, as she said, "I ate." "I" am the one who sinned. And who suffered for this sin? The woman.

> I will greatly multiply your pain in childbirth, in
> pain you will bring forth children; yet your desire
> will be for your husband, and he will rule over you.

The direct consequence of the woman's sin was multiplied pain, suffering. But the consequence of her sin was more devastating than just suffering. Because of her sin, in the marriage relationship, there would always be a separation.

> And he will rule over you.

In the relationship where she would most desire intimacy, in the relationship God designed to be the most intimate of all human relationships, she would find a separation. This— "and he will rule over you" —was not the creative design or plan of God before sin entered, and it is not God's intent for your marriage or mine today. It's the result of sin. It was not only the first woman who suffered for this sin. All women, all men, and all marriages since then suffer the same consequences of her sin and our sins: suffering and separation.

Then, the man sinned, as he said, "I ate." "I" am the one who sinned. And who suffered for this sin? The man.

> Because you have listened to the voice of your wife, and have eaten from the tree about which I commanded you, saying, "You shall not eat from it," cursed is the ground because of you. In toil you will eat of it all the days of your life. Both thorns and thistles it shall grow for you, and you will eat the plants of the field. By the sweat of your face you will eat bread, till you return to the ground, because from it you were taken, for you are dust, and to dust you shall return.
>
> Genesis 3.17-19

The immediate consequences of the man's sin were toil and sweat all the days of his life. But there was another consequence of his sin far more terrible: the end of life; death. "For you are dust, and to dust you shall return." While the consequence of the woman's sin was separation in relationships during life, the consequence of the man's sin was the ultimate separation from all relationships: death. Separation is always a consequence of sin, and death is the ultimate separation caused by sin. But it was not only the first man who suffered for this sin. All men and all women since then suffer the same consequences of his sin and our sins: toil and sweat all the days of our lives, and then death. The man's sin resulted in the same two consequences: suffering (toil and sweat) and then death (the ultimate separation).

Not only mankind would suffer for the sin of the man. God said, "Cursed is the ground because of you." The ground, all God's creation, suffered the curse of the man's sin. All creation is no longer as God designed it, all very good. When sin entered, creation itself was cursed.

We suffer not only for our own sins but also for the sins of those around us, all the way back to the sins of the first man and woman. And all God's creation suffers the curse of sin with us. The vast majority of our daily suffering is the direct consequence of our own sin inflicted on us and on those around us. The remainder of our suffering is the result of what is sometimes called natural disasters like hurricanes, floods, disease, or physical disabilities (as if suffering were somehow natural). This suffering too is the result of sin. "Cursed is the ground because of you."

> For the creation was subjected to futility, not willingly but because of Him who subjected it, in hope that the creation itself also will be set free from its slavery to corruption into the freedom of the glory of the children of God. For we know that *the whole creation groans and suffers* the pains of childbirth together until now.
>
> Romans 8:20-22 (italics mine)

To summarize, the consequences of sin are always separation and suffering. We are real people who make real decisions that have real consequences. We suffer not only for our own sins but also for the sins of those around us. And thirdly, we also suffer because the ground itself, the whole creation, is cursed by sin. "The whole creation groans and suffers" natural disasters, disease and disabilities because of the curse of sin.

And so, because they understood the Scriptures, His disciples asked Jesus why the man was born blind. Is he suffering for his own sins or the sins of his parents? "Rabbi, who sinned, this man or his parents, that he would be born blind?"

> Jesus answered, "It was neither that this man sinned, nor his parents; but it was so that the works of God might be displayed in him."
>
> John 9:3

We have spent this time considering the consequences of sin—separation and suffering—because the explanation by Jesus of "the works of God" was given in the context of the disciples' question about the consequences of sin.

Why was this man born blind? Knowing his heart, "Jesus answered, 'It was neither that this man sinned, nor his parents.'" His blindness was a direct consequence not of his own sin or of his parents' sin, but of Adam's sin. "Cursed is the ground because of you." This man was born blind because "the whole creation groans and suffers" the curse of sin.

Although the disciples of Jesus correctly identified from Scripture the two most likely causes of the man's suffering, they could not see his heart when they supposed he was suffering for his own sin or his parents' sin. This was the same wrong thinking of the Pharisees, when, a little later, they made the direct accusation that he was born blind because of his own or his parents' sins. "You were *born* entirely in sins…" (John 9:34; italics mine). It is a dangerous thing to judge the heart of someone based on suffering in his life. (See God's condemnation of Job's friends. God's wrath was kindled against them because they implicitly accused Job of sin as the cause of his suffering. Job 42:7-9.)

This man's suffering "was so that *the works of God* might be *displayed* in him." (John 9:3) The operative word here for me is *displayed*. The purpose of Jesus was not to do a new or special work in this man's life but to display the ongoing works of God on earth. As Jesus said when He was accused of making Himself equal with God, "My Father is working until now, and I Myself am working" (John 5:17). Often unseen, God the Father "is working" in the world with God the Son. But in this blind man, at this moment, God chose to display openly and to record for us in Scripture the ongoing "works of God." Let's look at "the works of God" *displayed* in this man's life.

The first, and maybe the most obvious, work of God *displayed* in his life was healing. Jesus removed the blindness from his life, and he "came back seeing." Jesus relieved his suffering.

The second work of God *displayed* in his life was the restoration of his relationship with God:

Jesus heard that they had put him out, and finding him, He said, "Do you believe in the Son of Man?"

He answered, "Who is He, Lord, that I may believe in Him?"

Jesus said to him, "You have both seen Him, and He is the one who is talking with you."

And he said, "Lord, I believe." And he worshiped Him.

John 9:35-38

The consequences of sin are both suffering and separation. Jesus not only healed him and relieved his suffering, Jesus also *displayed* "the works of God" in him by reconciling him with God. This man came back into a correct relationship with Jesus; he believed the *Word* of Jesus and worshipped Jesus. "And he said, 'Lord, I believe.' And he worshiped Him." Either Jesus is God, or Jesus condoned the man's blasphemy.

Where there was suffering, Jesus relieved the suffering and healed his blindness. Where there was separation, Jesus reconciled the relationship between the man and his God.

Jesus said this man was born "that the works of God might be displayed in him."

So were you, and so was I.

We were born to display the works of God in our lives. God longs to remove both sin and the consequences of sin from us. God longs to display His works of reconciliation and healing in each one of us.

I would like you to notice what Jesus did not say next. Jesus did not say, "I must work the works of Him who sent Me." Jesus said,

> "*We* must work the works of Him who sent Me."
>
> John 9:4 (italics mine)

While the response of Jesus to the suffering of the blind man was healing and reconciliation, the response of Jesus to the disciples' question about suffering was to call them to participate with Him in "*the works of God.*"

Are you reconciled with God? If not, the next chapter in this book is included especially for you. If so, you are called to participate with Jesus in the works of God:

> "*We* must work the works of Him who sent Me as long as it is day; night is coming when no one can work. While I am in the world, I am the Light of the world."
>
> John 9.4-5

If you have been reconciled with God, you are called to God's works of healing and reconciliation, to dealing with the consequences of sin on earth. *The Word of Reconciliation* has been entrusted to you (2 Corinthians 5:18-22).

"When He had said this, He spat on the ground, and made clay of the spittle, and applied the clay to his eyes, and said to him, 'Go, wash in the pool of Siloam' (which is translated, Sent). So he went away and washed, and came back seeing."

John 9:6-7

If you want to *see* "the works of God", that is, reconciliation and healing, in your own life, then *believe* the Word of Jesus and *obey*. That is what the blind man did:

After Jesus touched him, He said to him, "Go,   wash..."
and so he   went...   and washed,
and came back *seeing*."

Behold His glory.

THE WORD OF RECONCILIATION

God was in Christ reconciling the world to Himself, not counting their trespasses against them, and He has committed to us *the word of reconciliation*.

2 Corinthians 5:19 (italics mine)

I have written the notes you will find when you turn this page on a blackboard for different groups of young people. I have written them on a napkin sitting in a restaurant. I have shared them with teenagers in a park, with friends in their homes and with prisoners in their prison cells. I have explained them in two different languages and am always amazed how the Lord, by the power of His Spirit, uses a simple explanation of the gospel to lead many to believe. My greatest regret in life is that I have not been bold enough to share this message more often, for it is the power of God for salvation to everyone who believes (Romans 1:16).

God

He loves us.

> "For God so loved the world, that He gave His only begotten Son, that whoever believes in Him shall not perish, but have eternal life" (John 3:16).

He is holy and cannot accept anything less than 100 percent perfection.

> "Therefore, you are to be perfect, as your heavenly Father is perfect" (Matthew 5:48).

Man

We fall short of God's standard of 100 percent perfection.

> "For all have sinned and fall short of the glory of God" (Romans 3:23).

We are separated from God.

> "Behold, the LORD's hand is not so short that it cannot save; nor is His ear so dull that it cannot hear. But your iniquities have made a separation between you and your God, and your sins have hidden His face from you so that He does not hear" (Isaiah 59:1-2).

We face eternal separation, what the Bible calls death.

> "For the wages of sin is death" (Romans 6.23).

Jesus

Jesus Christ as a substitute, a double switch.

God offers us the death of Jesus on the cross as a substitute payment for our death penalty.

> "But God demonstrates His own love toward us, in that while we were yet sinners, *Christ died for us*" (Romans 5:8; italics mine).

God offers us the perfect righteousness of Jesus in exchange for our sinfulness.

> "He (*God*) made Him (*Jesus Christ*) who knew no sin to be sin on our behalf, so that we might become the righteousness of God in Him (*in Christ*)." 2 Corinthians 5:21 (added words in italics mine)

You

God provided a substitute and offers reconciliation to us.

The choice is ours: to remain separated from God by our sins *or* to receive Jesus Christ's death and righteousness as a gift from God and be reconciled with God.

> "But as many as received Him (*Jesus*), to them He gave the right to become children of God, even to those who believe in His name *(the name of Jesus)* (John 1:12, added words in italics mine).

If you feel far from God right now, there is something you need to know more than anything else – how much God loves you. "For God so loved the world, that He gave His only begotten son, that whoever believes in Him should not perish, but have eternal life."

Years ago someone read this Bible verse to me and asked me, "Where do you live? Do you live in the world?" I replied yes. "Are you somebody? Are you included in whoever?" I answered yes again. "If this includes you," he continued, "go ahead and read it like it was written to you by inserting your name into the verse." So I read, for God so loved Dennis that He gave His only begotten son, that if Dennis believes in Him, Dennis will not perish, but have eternal life. I encourage you to stop right now and read this verse again out loud using your name. Listen to what it sounds like. You are the one God loves.

On one occasion I was explaining to a group of young people how much God loves them and my son was sitting in the group. I told them that while I loved them, there was no one in the group that I loved enough to sacrifice my own son for. In fact, I cannot imagine loving anyone enough that I would sacrifice my son for them. I love my son so much I would sacrifice myself for him. Because of the way I love my son, it is beyond my comprehension that God could love you and me enough to sacrifice His Son for us. If you don't understand how much God loves you, you have missed a great message of the Bible. God loves you and wants you to be with Him.

But there is something else you need to know about God. He is holy and cannot accept anything less than 100% perfection. Jesus said, "Therefore you are to be perfect, as your heavenly Father is perfect." Jesus Himself said that, not me. God's standard of righteousness is 100% perfection. God is so holy that He cannot accept anything less than 100% perfect righteousness into His presence.

Are you perfect? Me neither. We fall short of God's standard of 100% perfection. The Bible says, "For all have sinned and fall short of the glory of God." That may be the most useless verse in the whole Bible for me. God doesn't have to tell me I'm a sinner. I already know very well that I am far from perfect. I have sinned and fall far short of God's standard of perfect righteousness. And according to that verse, so have you.

Because of our sin, we are separated from God. For me, a prophet named Isaiah said it best, "Behold, the Lord's hand is not so short that it cannot save; nor is His ear so dull that it cannot hear. But your iniquities have made a separation between you and your God, and your sins have hidden His face from you, so that He does not hear." If you feel far from God, who moved? Not God. God is still there reaching out to you. In fact, there is no place you can go that God cannot reach you. His hand is not so short that it cannot save you no matter where you are or what you have done. His ear is not so dull that it cannot hear you. You can't run far enough away from God that He cannot reach you or hear you. If you feel far from God right now, it is because you have turned your back on Him. You have separated yourself from God by your sin and you have hidden His face from you by turning away from Him. But He still sees you. And if God cannot hear you, it is only because you are not calling out to Him.

As bad as it is to be separated from God right now, sin has a consequence far more terrible. Not only does our sin separate us from God now, it puts us in danger of permanent separation from the presence of God, what the Bible calls death. The wages of sin is death. I'm so glad God isn't fair with me. Because if God gave me what I deserve, I'd be dead right now. The wages of sin is death. Rather than treating us fairly, what God offers us is love, forgiveness, patience and mercy. If you are separated from God, right now God is calling you to come to Him. Can you hear Him? If you turn your back on God, you have not only separated yourself from God, you are in danger of eternal separation, death.

That's the score. God loves us, but He is holy and cannot accept anything less than 100% perfect righteousness. We do not meet God's standard. No one is perfect. So not only are we separated from God, but we face eternal separation – death.

God's solution to our separation from Him was to offer His own Son, Jesus, to become our substitute in two important ways. First, God offers us the death of Jesus on the cross as a substitute payment for our death penalty. "But God demonstrates His own love toward us, in that while we were yet sinners, *Christ died for us*" (Romans 5:8; italics mine). God loves us so much that He didn't wait for us to come to Him.

While we were still sinners in rebellion against God, hating God and turned away from God, that is when God sent Jesus to be our substitute. I'm so glad God didn't wait for me to come to Him, because it never would have happened. God reached out to us while we were still sinners.

The good news of the gospel can be summed up in four words – *"Christ died for us"*. That is the heart of the gospel. "The wages of sin is death", but "Christ died for us". While we were still His enemies, God offered the death of His own son, Jesus, as a substitute for our death penalty. That is love.

But God not only offers us the death of Jesus on the cross as a substitute payment for our death penalty. God also offers us the perfect righteousness of Jesus in exchange for our sinfulness.

> For the love of Christ controls us, having concluded this, that one died for all, therefore all died; and He died for all, so that they who live might no longer live for themselves, but for Him who died and rose again on their behalf…Therefore if anyone is *in Christ*, he is a new creature; the old things passed away; behold, new things have come. Now all these things are from God, who reconciled us to Himself through Christ and gave us the ministry of reconciliation, namely, that God was in Christ reconciling the world to Himself, not counting their trespasses against them, and He has committed to us the *word of reconciliation*. Therefore, we are ambassadors for Christ, as though God were making an

appeal through us; we beg you on behalf of Christ, be reconciled to God. He (*God*) made Him (*Jesus Christ*) who knew no sin to be sin on our behalf, so that we might become the righteousness of God in Him (*in Christ*).

2 Corinthians 5:14-21
(added words in italics mine)

About two thousand years ago, God looked down from heaven on a cross at the place of a skull, which is translated *Golgotha*. Do you know what God saw hanging on that cross? God saw your sins and my sins. "He (*God*) made Him (*Jesus Christ*) who knew no sin to be sin on our behalf." And when God saw your sins and my sins on that cross, God treated Jesus like you and I deserve to be treated. God turned His back on Jesus and let Him suffer and die because those are the consequences of sin: suffering and separation.

Years ago, as a boy, I believed the Gospel that Jesus Christ died for me, and I asked Jesus to be my substitute so that His death would count for my sins. At the moment I believed the *Word* of Jesus that Jesus is who He said He is and that He died for me, I was reconciled with my God. My sin separating me from God was removed.

Now that I believe in Jesus, I am *in Christ*. When God looks down from heaven at me, do you know what He sees? Not my sins. God saw my sins on that cross two thousand years ago when He treated Jesus like I deserve to be treated. When God looks down at me today, God sees only the righteousness of Jesus because I am *in Christ*, and God treats me like only Jesus deserves to be treated. God receives me as His child. Christ became my substitute and died for me that I "might become the righteousness of God *in Him*" and be reconciled with God. But as many as received Him (*Jesus*), to them He gave the right to become children of God, even to those who believe in His name (*the name of Jesus*)(John 1:12; italics mine).

Before you finish reading this page, you will already have made a decision either to remain separated from God or to receive the death and righteousness of Jesus as a gift and become a child of God. If you accept the Word of Jesus that He is God the Son and that He died for you, but you have never told Jesus you believe in Him, why not tell Him now? Whoever you are, wherever you are, no matter what your sins or what you have done, at this moment Jesus can hear you. The words you use are not important. There is no magic formula or prayer. What matters is only your faith in Jesus. But if the following prayer expresses the desire of your heart, read it out loud to Jesus. Now is the time to bow your head and confess with your mouth to Jesus that you believe in Him.

> Jesus, thank you for loving me. I know I am a sinner separated from you. I don't want to die for my sins. Thank you for dying on the cross. Jesus, I want your death to count for my sins. I accept You, Jesus, as my substitute. Thank you for forgiving me. Thank you for making me a child of God. Come into my life and make me the man or woman you want me to be. Amen.

If you asked Jesus to be your substitute, Jesus is trustworthy. You are now in Christ, and the Bible says you have new hope (Colossians 1:27) because:

> Your sins are forgiven (Colossians 1:13-14).
>
> You are a child of God (John 1:12).
>
> You have eternal life (John 3:16).
>
> You will someday see Jesus (1 John 3:2).

> Beloved, now we are children of God, and it has not appeared as yet what we will be. We know that when He appears, we will be like Him, because we will see Him just as He is.
>
> 1 John 3:2

Behold His glory.

If you just made a decision to be reconciled with God by faith in Jesus Christ, write today's date and time on the page below along with a short note. You might just say, "Today I accepted Jesus as my substitute and became a child of God." Sign your name to your note. Then tell someone who loves you that you now believe in Jesus and have accepted Jesus as your substitute. Start attending a church that loves Jesus and teaches the Bible, if you do not already, and ask your pastor how to follow Jesus and walk with Him.

THE WILL OF GOD

> The Lord is not slow about His promise, as some count slowness, but is patient toward you, not wishing for any to perish but for all to come to repentance.
>
> 2 Peter 3:9

One day, the revelation of Jesus Christ will complete God's will on earth and in heaven. It is worthwhile to take a moment to consider God's patience toward us today as it relates to sin and the consequences of sin: separation and suffering.

Skeptics have mocked that if God exists, and if He really loves us, why does He allow us to suffer? Maybe God doesn't love us enough to stop our suffering. Or if God does really love us, maybe suffering and evil are stronger than God so that He cannot stop our suffering.

The question of suffering is very real in our family. If God loves us, why does God allow children to be born with disabilities, and in particular, our children? If God really loves us, why would God allow a doctor to not recommend a medical treatment for our child, questioning if his life was worth it? If God loves us, why do our children face such pity and rejection in the world and sometimes even in the church? If God loves us, why does God allow suffering in our family caused by my personal failures, struggles, and sins? The confession on the cover of this book is my own. It is an accurate statement that Jesus Christ came into the world to save sinners, and I am certainly a prime example of a sinner. Yet Jesus had mercy on me in order to demonstrate His perfect patience toward anyone who will believe in Him for eternal life. (See 1 Timothy 1:15-17.)

When faced with real life, always remember that separation and suffering are not the will of God on earth or in heaven. They are neither God's design nor intent for us. Both are the result of sin:

> The LORD God said to the serpent, "*Because you have done this…*" Then to Adam He said, "*Because you…*"
>
> Genesis 3:14, 17 (italics mine)

The curse of sin, both separation and suffering, is *because you* and I and those around us sin. Our separation and suffering are the result of sin, both ours and Adam's. God never intended us to be separated from each other, and especially not from Him. God never intended and does not want us to suffer.

Never believe that you suffer because God does not love you enough to stop your suffering or that you suffer because He is not able stop your suffering. God's love for us is beyond our comprehension (Ephesians 3:14-21) and His promise to end all our suffering is as sure as His Word:

And I heard a loud voice from the throne, saying, "Behold, the tabernacle of God is among men, and He will dwell among them, and they shall be His people, and God Himself will be among them, and He will wipe away every tear from their eyes; and there will no longer be any death; there will no longer be any mourning, or crying, or pain; the first things have passed away."

And He who sits on the throne said, "Behold, I am making all things new." And He said, "Write, for these words are faithful and true."

Revelation 21:3-5

One day, God will permanently end the *separation* of His children from each other, and especially their separation from Him, which is the *curse* of sin: "He will dwell among them, and they shall be His people, and God Himself will be among them…and there will no longer be any death." We will no longer be separated from God. God Himself will dwell among us. And we will no longer be separated from each other by death.

One day, God will also permanently end the *suffering* of His children, which is the *curse* of sin: "He will wipe away every tear from their eyes; and there will no longer be any death; there will no longer be any mourning, or crying, or pain; the first things have passed away".

As scripture says, "There will no longer be any *curse*" (Revelation 22:3; italics mine).

When Jesus, God the Son, came to earth as a man, God gave us a taste of that future day when He will live among us and heal us. God bridged the separation between Himself and us. God Himself, God the Son, came and dwelt among us, and we beheld His glory and His works. As a man, Jesus came face to face with sin and the consequences of sin, both separation and suffering. Not just the cross, but the entire earthly ministry of Jesus dealt with the curse and the consequences of sin. For example:

> But the Pharisees went out and conspired against Him, as to how they might destroy Him. But Jesus, aware of this, withdrew from there. Many followed Him, and He healed them all...
>
> Matthew 12:14-15

Because of the Pharisees' desire to destroy Him, Jesus withdrew and separated Himself from them. But of those who followed Jesus and brought their suffering to Him, Scripture says, "He healed them all." Healing was a major emphasis of the entire earthly ministry of Jesus. While among us, God the Son ended suffering.

And when Jesus stood before the tomb of Lazarus and faced death, the ultimate separation caused by sin, "Jesus wept," and then He reconciled Lazarus with his family (John 11:35-44). I wonder if Jesus wept not only for Lazarus and his family but also for you and me when He saw in Lazarus the horrific consequences of sin in all our lives. Separation and suffering are not God's desire for us. Our separation and suffering give God no pleasure (Ezekiel 18:32).

If from the beginning of creation, separation and suffering were never God's plan or intent for us, if Jesus bridged the separation between God and man and healed suffering while on earth, if God's promise to us is to someday permanently end all separation and suffering, someone might well ask, *What is God waiting for? I'm suffering now. Why doesn't God end suffering now?*

Let's suppose for a moment that God willed to permanently end all suffering in the world at midnight tonight. To remove suffering permanently, God would have to remove not only all ongoing suffering but also all the causes of suffering, that is, all the sinners. If God permanently removed all suffering and all the causes of suffering from the world at midnight tonight, would you be here tomorrow?

———————————— ❧ ⬥ ❧ ————————————

Neither would I because you and I, we, are the cause of so much of the suffering in our own lives and in the lives of those around us.

Children of God by faith in Jesus Christ as our substitute have both forgiveness and an eternal hope to be with God forever. We wait expectantly with joy for the return of Jesus, when He will cleanse us from all sin and end all our separation and suffering. But for most of the world, the return of Jesus will mean something quite different:

Alas, you who are longing for the day of the LORD, for what purpose will the day of the LORD be to you? It will be darkness and not light; as when a man flees from a lion and a bear meets him, or goes home, leans his hand against the wall and a snake bites him. Will not the day of the LORD be darkness instead of light, even gloom with no brightness in it?

Amos 5:18-20

Most of the world does not hope for the return of Jesus, and when it happens, the return of Jesus will not be a joyful event for them:

I looked when He broke the sixth seal, and there was a great earthquake; and the sun became black as sackcloth made of hair, and the whole moon became like blood; and the stars of the sky fell to the earth, as a fig tree casts its unripe figs when shaken by a great wind. The sky was split apart like a scroll when it is rolled up, and every mountain and island were moved out of their places. Then the kings of the earth and the great men and the commanders and the rich and the strong and every slave and free man hid themselves in the caves and among the rocks of the mountains; and they said to the mountains and to the rocks, "Fall on us and hide us from the presence of Him who sits on the throne, and from the wrath of the Lamb; for the great day of their wrath has come, and who is able to stand?

Revelation 6:12-17

In the beginning, because of their sin,

> the man and his wife *hid themselves from the presence* of the LORD God.

Genesis 3:8 (italics mine)

In the end, because of their sin,

> the kings…the great men…the commanders…the rich…the strong…every slave and free man *hid themselves…from the presence* of Him who sits on the throne, and from the wrath of the Lamb.

Revelation 6:15-16 (italics mine)

The separation between God and man that began in the garden of Eden because of sin will culminate on earth when Jesus, God the Son, returns. We are real people who make real decisions that have real consequences. The consequences of sin are real.

For everyone who is not "in Christ," the day of the Lord will not be a joyful day of reconciliation with God and the removal of all suffering, when "He shall wipe away every tear from their eyes." Scripture says that on the day of the Lord, everyone who is not "in Christ" will face "the wrath of the Lamb." "And who is able to stand" in "the presence of Him who sits on the throne"? Not kings, not great men, not commanders, not the rich, not the strong; no sinner can stand in the presence of Holy God.

So what is God waiting for? Why doesn't God end all suffering now? The answer to this question lies within God's compassion and patience:

> The Lord is not slow about His promise, as some count slowness, but is patient toward you, not wishing for any to perish but for all to come to repentance.
>
> 2 Peter 3:9

God allows the suffering of His children not because He does not love us. He loves us enough to have sent His own Son to die for us (John 3:16). Neither do we suffer because God is not able to stop our suffering. One day, He will. But to remove all the suffering of His children, God will have to remove all sinners from His presence for all eternity. God only allows suffering to continue because of His patience and compassion, "not wishing for any to perish but for all to come to repentance."

In our suffering, we, as God's children, have a great privilege, the privilege to participate in the compassion of God for a lost world in danger of eternal separation from the presence of God. Paul put it this way:

Suffer hardship with me, as a good soldier of Christ Jesus…For this reason I endure all things for the sake of those who are chosen, so that they also may obtain the salvation which is in Christ Jesus and with it eternal glory.

2 Timothy 2:3 and 10

Paul encouraged Christ's followers to endure hardship and suffering "for the sake of those who are chosen, so that they also may obtain the salvation which is in Christ Jesus."

The great mystery about *the will of God* is not finding God's special, individual plan for your life but rather why God would allow His children to participate with Him in His eternal plan and to share the suffering and the "eternal glory" of Jesus.

God allows His children to suffer, as Jesus also suffered, because of His compassion for the lost, "that they also may obtain the salvation which is in Christ Jesus." While God allows His children to suffer on earth because of His compassion for the lost, God allowed His Son Jesus to suffer far more, to the point of death on a cross. For God's children, reconciled to Him by the blood of His Son Jesus, suffering is our opportunity and privilege to participate with God in His compassion for the lost.

Peter wrote,

For you have been called for this purpose, since Christ also suffered for you, leaving you an example for you to follow in His steps.

1 Peter 2:21; see 1 Peter 2:19-24

Beloved, do not be surprised at the fiery ordeal among you, which comes upon you for your testing, as though some strange thing were happening to you; but to the degree that you share the sufferings of Christ, keep on rejoicing, so that also at the revelation of His glory you may rejoice with exultation…Therefore, those also who suffer according to *the will of God* shall entrust their souls to a faithful Creator in doing what is right.

1 Peter 4:12-13, 19
(italics mine; see 1 Peter 4:12-19)

God's children suffer according to *the will of God*. Even though I don't like to suffer, I tend to draw closer to God and to depend more on Him while suffering than while I have abundance without pain. Suffering reminds me who I am, a created being and not a little god who is master of my own destiny. Maybe part of God's purpose in my suffering is to turn me back to dependence on my faithful Creator. "Therefore, those also who suffer according to *the will of God* shall entrust their souls to a faithful Creator in doing what is right". (1 Peter 4:19)

Paul wrote,

> The Spirit Himself testifies with our spirit that we
> are children of God, and if children, heirs also, heirs
> of God and fellow heirs with Christ, if indeed we
> suffer with Him so that we may also be glorified
> with Him."
>
> Romans 8:16-17

> For to you it has been granted for Christ's sake, not
> only to believe in Him, but also to suffer for His
> sake...
>
> Philippians 1:29, 27-30

Sharing the suffering of Jesus is part of someday sharing
the glory of God.

> Now I rejoice in my sufferings for your sake, and
> in my flesh I do my share on behalf of His body,
> which is the church, in filling up what is lacking in
> Christ's afflictions...that I might fully carry out the
> preaching of the word of God...which is, *Christ in
> you, the hope of glory.*
>
> Colossians 1:24-27

As children of God reconciled to Him by the death of
Jesus His Son, Christ in us is our hope of glory. Being in
Christ and having Christ in us is the reason for our hope
to share His eternal glory. For children of God, sharing the

suffering of Christ is part of sharing the hope of being glo-ried with Christ. Suffering is part of having *Christ in you, the hope of glory*. (Pause here and read John 15:18-21.)

> Indeed, all who desire to live godly in Christ Jesus will be persecuted.
>
> 2 Timothy 3:12

Our suffering and sharing in Christ's afflictions can be a source of joy for us, as it was for Paul (Colossians 1:24). In *the will of God*, our suffering is for the benefit of others, that the proclamation of the Word of God might be fully carried out before lost sinners are eternally separated from Christ and from all hope. When God allows His children to suffer momentarily on earth the consequences of sin, the eternal destiny of those who are lost without Christ hangs in the balance. We can rejoice that our suffering is for the benefit of those others so that the sharing of the good news of the gospel might be fully carried out.

> I rejoice in my sufferings for your sake…that I might fully carry out the preaching of the word of God…which is, *Christ in you, the hope of glory*.
>
> Colossians 1:24-27

Paul rejoiced in his suffering and saw in suffering the opportunity and privilege to participate with God in His compassion for the lost.

In his suffering, Job asked God, "Why?"

"Have I sinned? What have I done to you?"

Job 7:20

"Let me know why You contend with me."

Job 10:2 see also Job 3:20; 13:24; 19:21-22

It is instructive that God never offered Job an answer, but God did allow us to see that something far bigger than Job's suffering was going on. Satan had challenged, "Does Job fear God for nothing?" (Job 1:9). Job only serves God for what he can get from God, Satan accused. At its heart, Job's worship of God is self serving, not serving God. Satan was wrong about Job, who confessed tremendous faith in God.

Though He slay me, I will hope in Him."

Job 13:15

But was Satan right about me? Do I serve God selfishly only for what I want to get from God, to receive His blessing on earth and to obtain heaven? Or do I worship and serve God because He is God and He is worthy of my faith, obedience, and worship no matter what happens to me?

In the end, God's response to Job was not an answer to his question, "Why?" but a series of questions that began like this:

Then the LORD answered Job out of the storm and said, "Now gird up your loins like a man; I will ask you, and you instruct Me. Will you really annul My judgment? Will you condemn Me that you may be justified?"

Job 40:6-8

"Who are you, Job, to question or to challenge Me?" God asked.

My wife and I have three children with special needs. We hear many remarks about suffering and attempts by well-meaning Christians to somehow justify God or to explain God's purpose. Only God can ultimately answer the question, "Why?" Who am I to either explain or to question the will of God or the goodness of the will of God to give these children to our family?

On occasion when personal sickness or pain has become so intense that I no longer think clearly, my faith in the goodness of God rests on three affirmations:

- God loves me. Never doubt God's love in suffering.

- God is able. Never doubt that God can heal. He can and He will, even if He does not at the moment.

- God is glorified by my suffering. My suffering demonstrates and proclaims God's compassion and patience toward sinners. Were it not for God's patience toward the lost, I would not be suffering here and now.

As with Job, in my suffering there is something bigger going on than me. You and I are not the center. At the center is God's will, His glory and His compassion for the lost.

> To the degree that you share the sufferings of Christ, keep on rejoicing, so that also at the revelation of His glory you may rejoice with exultation"
>
> 1 Peter 4:13

> The Spirit Himself testifies with our spirit that we are children of God, and if children, heirs also, heirs of God and fellow heirs with Christ, if indeed we suffer with Him so that we may also be glorified with Him.
>
> Romans 8:16-17

Never doubt in the dark what you've seen in the light. If you are suffering right now as a child of God, do not despair or doubt God's steadfast love for you. And remember that along with His compassion for the lost, God has compassion on His children. Look for the goodness of the Lord, and wait for Him.

When I have nothing else left to hang on to, I cling to the Lord and to His Word. When my heart is breaking, I search God's Word, especially the Psalms, for a glimpse of Him. For over three thousand years, the people of God have found comfort and encouragement in the Psalms, which are songs from the heart of men like King David. The following verses have spoken the Lord's comfort and encouragement to me. I offer them only as a place for you to start looking in God's Word if you are suffering right now. As you search the Psalms and all of God's Word for yourself, the Lord will meet you where you are and show you verses different from these that will speak His comfort and encouragement to you. But these speak to me:

> Just as a father has compassion on his children, so the Lord has compassion on those who fear Him. For He Himself knows our frame; He is mindful that we are but dust.
>
> Psalm 103:13-14

> I would have despaired unless I had believed that I would see the goodness of the Lord in the land of the living. Wait for the Lord; be strong and let your heart take courage; yes, wait for the Lord.
>
> Psalm 27:13-14 (See also Psalm 94:12-14.)

> The Lord's lovingkindnesses indeed never cease, for His compassions never fail. They are new every morning; great is Your faithfulness…The Lord is good to those who wait for Him, to the person who seeks Him.
>
> Lamentations 3:21-25

For just as the sufferings of Christ are ours in abundance, so also our comfort is abundant through Christ.

2 Corinthians 1:5, see 3-7

Therefore we do not lose heart...For momentary, light affliction is producing for us an eternal weight of glory far beyond all comparison...

2 Corinthians 4:16-18

I have been young and now I am old, yet I have not seen the righteous forsaken...For the LORD loves justice and does not forsake His godly ones...

Psalm 37:25-28

My sheep hear My voice, and I know them, and they follow Me; and I give eternal life to them, and they will never perish; and no one will snatch them out of My hand.

John 10:27-28

And so, God's children wait and pray:

Our Father who art in heaven, hallowed be Thy name. Thy kingdom come. Thy will be done, on earth as it is in heaven...

Matthew 6:9-10 (KJV)

The Lord is not slow about His promise, as some count slowness, but is patient toward you, not wishing for any to perish but for all to come to repentance.

2 Peter 3:9

The great mystery about *the will of God* is why God would allow His children to participate with Him in His eternal plan and to share the suffering of Jesus so that we will also share His eternal glory. For God's children, reconciled to Him by the blood of His Son, Jesus, suffering is our opportunity and privilege to participate with God in His compassion for the lost.

Christ *in you*, the hope of glory.

And when suffering comes into your life,

Behold His glory *in you*.

THE WORSHIP OF GOD AT THE REVELATION OF JESUS CHRIST

"And behold, I am coming quickly. Blessed is he who heeds the words of the prophecy of this book." I, John, am the one who heard and saw these things. And when I heard and saw, I fell down to worship at the feet of the angel who showed me these things. But he said to me, "Do not do that. I am a fellow servant of yours and of your brethren the prophets and of those who heed the words of this book. *Worship God.*"

Revelation 22:7-9 (italics mine)

In the beginning, God revealed Himself through the goodness of His creation. The Old Testament prophets progressively revealed God's *Promise* of the coming of Jesus. At the birth of Jesus, God revealed His *Gospel* message that a Savior who is Christ the Lord is born for us. While on earth, Jesus claimed to be God the Son, the revelation of God Himself born as a man. As the *Son of God*, Jesus revealed the *Work of God* on earth and offered *Reconciliation* with God through His sacrifice on the cross. Through His life, death, and resurrection, Jesus revealed the *Will of God* for everyone who believes in Him.

The book of the Revelation of Jesus Christ stands at the end of the Bible as the completion of the revelation of Jesus Christ through all of Scripture. While the phrase, "the Revelation of Jesus Christ" (Revelation 1:1) is correctly understood as the revelation *from* Jesus Christ (Revelation 22:16), it is more than this. "The Revelation of Jesus Christ" is the final revelation *from* Jesus of *who* Jesus Christ *is*.[11] "The Revelation of Jesus Christ" completes for us God's revelation of Himself in and through Jesus Christ.

> Do not be afraid; I am the first and the last, and *the living One*; and I was dead, and behold, I am alive forevermore, and I have the keys of death and of Hades. Therefore write the things which you have seen, and the things which are, and the things which will take place after these things.
>
> Revelation 1:17-19 (italics mine)

Jesus Himself, "*the living One*," gives John a three-part outline of the revelation of *who* Jesus Christ *is*. Jesus tells John,

"Therefore, write the things which you have seen, and the things which are, and the things which will take place after these things."

Revelation 1:19

Jesus instructed John to introduce the final revealing of Himself by reviewing for us what John personally had already seen and knew about Jesus, "write the things which you have seen," as opposed to the things I am about to show you. It seems to me that Jesus requested John to begin by summarizing for us the most important things he learned about Jesus while following Jesus on earth as a disciple. And this is, in fact, how John began the revelation of who Jesus is with a review in Revelation 1:5-6 of the life and work of Jesus on earth.

John saw Jesus revealed during His life on earth as:

- a faithful witness, the truth (John 14:8-10 and 18:37; 1 Timothy 6:13)

- the firstborn of the dead, resurrected (John 20:8-9; Colossians 1:18-20)

- the ruler of the kings of the earth, with authority (John 17:2, 18:37, 19:11; Matthew 28:18; Colossians 1:16; 1 Timothy 6:14-16)

- He who loves us (John 15:12-13)

- He who released us from our sins, He died for us (John 19:17, Romans 5:8)

- He who made us to be a kingdom; see the kingdom of Heaven in all of Matthew (Mark 14:25, Revelation 5:9-10)

- He who made us priests to His God and Father:
  - priests as intercessors by prayer and witness (Hebrews 7:23-25; 2 Corinthians 5:20-21)
  - priests as those who lead in worship (Hebrews 9:6)

- He who is worthy of glory and dominion forever and ever (Matthew 16:27 and 25:31, Romans 11:36, Ephesians 3:20-21, 1 Peter 4:11)

The second part of the revelation of *who* Jesus Christ *is* concerns "the things which are." What follows in the text is a picture of Jesus among the churches and a description of how Jesus reveals Himself to each church (Revelation 1:12 to 3:22). As Jesus reveals Himself to each church, He gives each church a challenge and makes a promise to him who overcomes (see 1 John 5:4-5). The revelation of "the things which are" describes how Jesus reveals Himself today by the Holy Spirit within His church to believers and through His church to the world.

The final part of the revelation of *who* Jesus Christ *is* concerns "the things which will take place after these things," that is, how Jesus will be revealed someday in the future (Revelation 4:1 to 22:5). The word *throne* appears twice in Revelation 4:2 and a total of thirty-eight times from here to the end of the revelation. "The throne of God and of the Lamb" (Revelation 22:1) is the focal point of the revelation of *who* Jesus Christ *is* in the things to come. The authority of Jesus (John 5:22-23), His worthiness (Revelation 5:12), and His glory (Revelation 5:13) will only be fully revealed from the throne.

In Revelation 5, Jesus is revealed standing before the throne as the only One in heaven worthy to unseal the judgment and the wrath of God against sin and sinners (see John 5:22-23, 2 Timothy 4:1). It is Jesus the Lamb, standing as if slain, who unseals the book of the judgment and wrath of God. From this point on through the remainder of the Revelation, as Jesus breaks each seal, as each trumpet sounds, and as each bowl of the wrath of God is poured out, John is allowed to see both the results *on earth* and the response *in heaven* to God's wrath against sin and sinners.

On earth:

> The rest of mankind, who were not killed by these plagues, *did not repent* of the works of their hands, so as not to worship demons, and the idols of gold and of silver and of brass and of stone and of wood, which can neither see nor hear nor walk; and they *did not repent* of their murders nor of their sorceries nor of their immorality nor of their thefts.
>
> Revelation 9:20-21 (italics mine)

On earth:

> Men were scorched with fierce heat; and they blasphemed the name of God who has the power over these plagues, and they *did not repent* so as to give Him glory…and they blasphemed the God of heaven because of their pains and their sores; and they *did not repent* of their deeds.

> Revelation 16:9 and 11 (italics mine)

On earth:

> Then the kings of the earth and the great men and the commanders and the rich and the strong and every slave and free man hid themselves in the caves and among the rocks of the mountains; and they said to the mountains and to the rocks, "Fall on us and hide us from the presence of Him who sits on the throne, and from the wrath of the Lamb; for the great day of their wrath has come, and who is able to stand?"

> Revelation 6:15-17

When *unrepentant* sinners see the revelation of the wrath of the Lamb and of Him who sits on the throne, there will be no place to stand and no place to hide from the righteous wrath of Jesus (Revelation 2:6).

> "… for the great day of their wrath has come, and who is able to stand?"

> Revelation 6:17; Malachi 3:2

The answer to this question is important. "Who is able to stand" during the wrath of the Lamb and of Him who sits on the throne? John's vision continues in the next verse:

> After this I saw four angels *standing* at the four corners of the earth, holding back the four winds of the earth, so that no wind would blow on the earth or on the sea or on any tree.
>
> Revelation 7:1 (italics mine)

On earth, angels who serve the Lamb will *stand* during the wrath of the Lamb and of Him who sits on the throne.

In heaven, those who worship the Lamb will *stand* before the throne and around the throne.

> After these things I looked, and behold, a great multitude which no one could count, from every nation and all tribes and peoples and tongues, *standing before the throne* and before the Lamb, clothed in white robes, and palm branches were in their hands; and they cry out with a loud voice, saying, "Salvation to our God who sits on the throne, and to the Lamb." And all the angels *were standing around the throne* and around the elders and the four living creatures; and they fell on their faces before the throne and *worshiped God*, saying, "Amen, blessing and glory and wisdom and thanksgiving and honor and power and might, be to our God forever and ever. Amen."
>
> Revelation 7:9-12 (italics mine)

The only ones "*able to stand*" during the wrath of the Lamb and the wrath of Him who sits on the throne will be those who serve Him and those who worship "before the throne and before the Lamb." Will you be able to stand?

The Revelation of Jesus Christ is a book about the worship of God. The word *worship* appears twenty-four times in the revelation of *who* Jesus Christ *is*, more times than in any other book of the Bible. In contrast to the worship of the beast, the dragon and demons, and the final end of that worship[12], the Revelation of Jesus Christ describes the final end of worshiping "before the throne and before the Lamb" and calls us to worship God who sits on the throne and the Lamb.

Stated simply, worship is attributing worth to God. Worship is describing or declaring to God His worth and why He is worthy:

> The twenty-four elders will fall down before Him who sits on the throne, and *will worship Him* who lives forever and ever, and will cast their crowns before the throne, saying, "*Worthy are You*, our Lord and our God, to receive glory and honor and power; for You created all things, and because of Your will they existed, and were created."
>
> Revelation 4:10-11 (italics mine)

They "*will worship Him*" saying, "*Worthy are You*." In its essence, worship is no more and no less than expressing to God, "You are worthy."

Our Lord and our God, You are worthy to receive glory and honor and power because You sit on the throne, because You live forever, because You created all things, and because of Your will all things exist.

Revelation 4:10-11 lays out a pattern of worship that consists of four elements of attributing worth to God.

Four elements of worship:	Example of worship
	in Revelation 4:10–11
1. Title of the One who is worthy	Our Lord and our God
2. Statement of worth – You are worthy	worthy are You
3. Worth of the One worshiped – (of) or to receive:	glory and honor and power
4. Reason One is worthy – because:	You sit on the throne You live forever You created all things by Your will all things exist

This is the pattern of worship throughout the Revelation of Jesus Christ that can be observed in the expressions of worship as they crescendo from Revelation chapter 4 toward the climax of the revelation of *who* Jesus *is*. As the wrath of God who sits on the throne and the wrath of the Lamb toward sin and sinners is poured out *on earth*, the response *in heaven* is a growing crescendo of worship "before the throne and before the Lamb."

The Revelation of Jesus Christ is a call to worship. Look at each of the following expressions of worship in the order in which they appear from Revelation chapter 4 through chapter 21. Consider each expression of worship as both an example and a call to worship. Heed the words of this book. Worship God (Revelation 1:3; 22:9).

When the four living creatures worship the Lord God, they attribute holiness to Him because He was and is and is to come the Almighty:

> Holy, holy, holy is the Lord God, the Almighty,
> who was and who is and who is to come.
>
> Revelation 4:8

Pattern: The Lord God is worthy of His holiness because He was and is and is to come the Almighty One.

When the twenty-four elders worship God, they attribute glory, honor, and power to Him because He created all things and because of His will:

Worthy are You, our Lord and our God, *to receive* glory and honor and power; for You created all things, and because of Your will they existed, and were created.

Revelation 4:11 (italics mine)

Pattern: Our Lord and God, You are worthy to receive Your glory and honor and power because You created all things, and because of Your will, they existed and were created.

When they sing a new song, they worship the Lamb, saying that He is worthy to take the book and to break its seals because He was slain:

Worthy are You to take the book and to break its seals; for You were slain, and purchased for God with Your blood men from every tribe and tongue and people and nation. You have made them to be a kingdom and priests to our God; and they will reign upon the earth.

Revelation 5:9-10 (italics mine)

Pattern: Lamb of God, *You are worthy* to unseal the judgment and wrath of God against sinners because You were slain and because You purchased for God with Your blood men from every tribe, tongue, people, and nation to be a kingdom and priests to our God and to reign on the earth.

When the angels worship the Lamb, they attribute power, riches, wisdom, might, honor, glory, and blessing to Him because He was slain:

> *Worthy* is the Lamb that was slain *to receive* power and riches and wisdom and might and honor and glory and blessing.
>
> > (Revelation 5:12; italics mine).

Pattern: Lamb of God, You are *worthy to receive* Your power, riches, wisdom, might, honor, glory, and blessing because You were slain.

When every created thing in heaven and on earth worships God and the Lamb, they attribute to them blessing, honor, glory, and eternal dominion because God sits on the throne:

> To Him who sits on the throne, and to the Lamb, be blessing and honor and glory and dominion forever and ever.
>
> > Revelation 5:13

Pattern: God and Lamb of God, You are worthy of Your blessing, honor, glory, and eternal dominion because You sit on the throne.

When a great multitude that no one can count, from every nation and all tribes and peoples and tongues, worships God and the Lamb, they attribute to God and the Lamb salvation because God sits on the throne:

Salvation to our God who sits on the throne, and
to the Lamb.

Revelation 7:10

Pattern: God and Lamb of God, You are worthy of Your salvation because You sit on the throne.

When the twenty-four elders who sit on their thrones
before God fall down on their faces and worship God, they
thank God because He is almighty, eternal, and has begun
to reign:

> We give You thanks, O Lord God, the Almighty,
> who are and who were, *because* You have taken
> Your great power and have begun to reign. And
> the nations were enraged, and Your wrath came,
> and the time came for the dead to be judged, and
> the time to reward Your bond-servants the proph-
> ets and the saints and those who fear Your name,
> the small and the great, and to destroy those who
> destroy the earth.
>
> Revelation 11:17-18 (italics mine)

Pattern: O Lord God, You are worthy of our thanks and of
our fear of Your name *because* You are almighty and eternal
and because with Your wrath, judgment, reward, and destruction You have begun to reign.

An angel preached an eternal gospel to those who live
on earth, to every nation, tribe, tongue, and people, to

worship God with fear, giving Him glory because He made the heaven, earth, sea, and springs of water and because the hour of His judgment has come:

> Fear God, and give Him glory, *because* the hour of His judgment has come; worship Him who made the heaven and the earth and sea and springs of waters.
>
> Revelation 14:7 (italics mine)

Pattern: God, You are worthy of our fear and of our worship and of Your glory because You made heaven, earth, sea, and springs of water and *because* the hour of Your judgment has come.

When those who have been victorious over the beast worship God, they will sing the song of Moses and the song of the Lamb, saying, "Who will not fear, O Lord, and glorify Your name for You alone are holy and Your righteous acts have been revealed?"

> Great and marvelous are Your works, O Lord God, the Almighty; righteous and true are Your ways, King of the nations! Who will not fear, O Lord, and glorify Your name? For You alone are holy; for all the nations will come and worship before you, for your righteous acts have been revealed.
>
> Revelation 15:2-4

Pattern: O Lord God, You are worthy of our fear and of the glory of Your name because You are the Almighty, the King of the Nations, and because You alone are holy and because Your righteous acts have been revealed. Because Your works are great and marvelous, and because Your ways are righteous and true, all the nations will come and worship before You.

When a great multitude in heaven worships God, they will praise His salvation, glory, and power because His judgments are true and righteous:

> Hallelujah! Salvation and glory and power belong to our God; *because* his judgments are true and righteous; for He has judged the great harlot who was corrupting the earth with her immorality, and he has avenged the blood of his bond-servants on her.
>
> Revelation 19:1-2 (italics mine)

Pattern: Our God, You are worthy of our praise and of Your salvation, glory, and power because Your judgments are true and righteous and because You have judged and avenged.

When the twenty-four elders and the four living creatures fall down and worship God who sits on the throne, they will praise Him:

> Amen. Hallelujah!
>
> Revelation 19:4

Pattern: God, You are worthy of our praise because You sit on the throne.

"Amen," which means "May it be so," that You sit on the throne.

"Hallelujah," which means "Praise the Lord!" that You sit on the throne.

When all His bond-servants with the voice of a great multitude worship the Lord our God, they will praise and glorify Him because He is almighty, because He reigns, and because the marriage of the Lamb has come and His bride is ready:

> Hallelujah! For the Lord our God, the Almighty, reigns. Let us rejoice and be glad and give the glory to Him, for the marriage of the Lamb has come and His bride has made herself ready.
>
> Revelation 19:6-7

Pattern: Lord our God, You are worthy of our praise, rejoicing and gladness and of Your glory because You are almighty, because You reign and because the marriage of the Lamb has come and Your bride is ready (Revelation 21:9-10).

Within the pattern of worship observed in the previous twelve examples, the *acts* of worship include fear, praise, glory, honor, thanks, blessing, rejoicing, and gladness (Revelation 4:9, 7:12, 11:17, 14:7, 15:4, 19:1, 5-7), saying or crying out with a loud voice (Revelation 4:10, 5:12-14, 7:10-12, 11:15-17, 15:3-4, 19:1-6), casting crowns (Revelation

4:10), singing a song (Revelation 15:3-4), falling down on their faces (Revelation 4:10, 5:14, 7:11, 11:16, 19:4), and standing clothed in white robes (Revelation 7:9, 13-14). The Revelation of Jesus Christ, that is, the revealing of *who* Jesus *is*, will result in the worship of God.

Some of the worship described in the Revelation of Jesus Christ is false worship. (See endnote 12.) At two points, even John is tempted to worship someone or something less than God Himself. At both times, we hear the same command, "Worship God," which is the central imperative, the call to action in the Revelation of Jesus Christ (Revelation 19:10, 22:9).

"In the beginning, God…" (Genesis 1:1) All Scripture begins in Genesis with this affirmation that the God of the Bible is the source of all things and that everything we see and know, all reality, *begins with* and comes from Him. All Scripture ends in the Revelation of Jesus Christ with a call to worship the God revealed through all of Scripture as God the Son, Jesus Christ, the Lamb of God who takes away the sin of the world. All Scripture from Genesis to Revelation is a call to know our God, to believe our God, and to worship our God.

The Bible ends with these words: "The grace of the Lord Jesus be with all. Amen" (Revelation 22:21). The last message God leaves with us in Scripture is His desire that we all know and experience not "the wrath of the Lamb" but "the grace of the Lord Jesus," of "Him who loves us and released us from our sins by His blood" (Revelation 1:5). God's grace, that is, God's benefit bestowed on those who are unworthy of it, is that we can know Him and be reconciled to Him and be healed by Him because He loves us and sent Jesus as a substitute to die for our sins (1 Corinthians 15:3). Is it possible to begin to comprehend the magnitude of God's grace without a glimpse of just how much God hates sin ("the wrath of the Lamb")? I think not. Only as we read the Revelation of Jesus Christ and begin to understand how much God and the Lamb of God hate sin (Romans 1:18-21) can we begin to comprehend the magnitude of God's grace toward sinners and how much He loves us.

The Revelation of Jesus Christ is about wrath and worship. As we see how much God hates sin, the Revelation of *who* Jesus Christ *is* calls us to worship the Lamb of God who takes away the sin of the world, who was slain for sin because He loves us, and who now sits on the throne with God as our God.

Consider carefully the following summary of the worship of God as described in the Revelation of Jesus Christ. "Heed the words of this book" (Revelation 1:3; 19:10; 22:9) and with those "who hold the testimony of Jesus; worship God":

Lamb of God, God on the throne,

You are Worthy
to receive our fear, praise, thanks, service, obedience, rejoicing and gladness,

to receive Your salvation, glory, honor, wisdom, power, blessing, might and dominion, *to receive* the worship of all the nations before You,

because You are holy, righteous and almighty,

because You were and are and are to come,

because You created all things, and *because* of Your will they exist,

because You were slain, and *because* You purchased for God with Your blood men from every tribe and tongue and people and nation. You have made them to be a kingdom and priests to our God; and they will reign upon the earth,

because You will sit on the throne and reign,

because You will take Your great power and reign. Your wrath will come, and the time will come for the dead to be judged, and the time to reward Your bond-servants the prophets and the saints and those who fear Your name, and to destroy those who destroy the earth.

because You made heaven, earth, sea and springs of water,

because the hour of Your judgment will come,

because You are the Almighty, the King of the Nations,

because You alone are holy,

because Your righteous acts are revealed,

because Your works are great and marvelous,

because Your ways are righteous and true,

because Your judgments are true and righteous,

because You will judge and avenge,

because You are holy and righteous,

because You will reign with your wrath, judgment and reward,

because the marriage of the Lamb will come and Your bride, those who are Yours, will be ready.

> But God demonstrates His own love toward us, in that while we were yet sinners, Christ died for us...we shall be saved from the wrath of God through Him.
>
> Romans 5:8-9

When the great day of the revealing of the Lord, Jesus Christ comes, where will you be? Calling out for Jesus to come, worshiping "before the throne and before the lamb," or separated from the presence of Him who sits on the throne and facing "the wrath of the Lamb"?

The Revelation of Jesus Christ is a revelation of *who* Jesus Christ *is* and a call to worship Him. John's response to the Revelation of Jesus Christ was worship:

> I, John, am the one who heard and saw these things. And when I heard and saw, I fell down to worship...
>
> Revelation 22:8

Overwhelmed by the revealing of who Jesus is, John fell down before the angelic messenger to worship. Twice the messenger reminded John that the focus of his worship should not be the messenger of the revelation, but Jesus, the One revealed (Revelation 19:10; 22:9).

The message of the Revelation of *who* Jesus Christ *is* promises a blessing to all those who heed the words of this book (Revelation 1:3; 22:7). As summarized in Revelation

19:10 and 22:9, the heart of the message of the Revelation of Jesus Christ from "those who heed the words of this book" is:

Worship God.

The greatest blessing or benefit available to all of God's creation, including God's children by grace, is to know, to believe, and to worship our God, Jesus Christ.

> "I, Jesus, have sent My angel to testify to you these things for the churches. I am the root and the descendant of David (*the Promise of God*), the bright morning star."
>
> The Spirit and the bride say, "Come." And let the one who hears say, "Come." And let the one who is thirsty come; let the one who wishes take the water of life without cost…
>
> He who testifies to these things says, "Yes, I am coming quickly." Amen. Come, Lord Jesus.
>
> Revelation 22:16-17, 20
(added phrase in italics mine)

And so, God's children by His sovereign grace wait and pray:

> Our Father, who art in heaven, hallowed be Thy name. Thy kingdom come…

Come, Lord Jesus.

> For Thine is the kingdom, and the power, and the *glory*, forever. Amen.
>
> Matthew 6:9-13; 1 Chronicles 29:11;
> Revelation 5:13

Behold His glory.

PATHS OF
RIGHTEOUSNESS

> He leadeth me in the *paths of righteousness* for his
> name's sake.
>
> Psalm 23:3 (italics mine)

Jesus, the Lamb of God, is worthy of our fear, praise, thanks, service, obedience, rejoicing, gladness, and worship. The final Revelation of Jesus Christ reveals Jesus as our transcendent God. If you miss this, you have missed a salient truth of the revelation of the glory of God in Jesus from Genesis to the final Revelation of who Jesus is.

On one occasion during a Bible study of the Book of Revelation, a close friend of mine commented that while he believes Jesus is our God, when he bows his head to pray, the image of Jesus that comes to his mind is not the one from Revelation of:

> one like a son of man, clothed in a robe reaching to the feet, and girded across His chest with a golden sash. His head and His hair were white like white

wool, like snow; and His eyes were like a flame of fire. His feet were like burnished bronze, when it has been made to glow in a furnace, and His voice was like the sound of many waters. In His right hand He held seven stars, and out of His mouth came a sharp two-edged sword; and His face was like the sun shining in its strength.

Revelation 1:13-16

When we think of Jesus, most of us do not envision a golden sash, white hair, flaming eyes, a sword coming out of His mouth and His face shining like the sun. We want to know Jesus personally as He is revealed in the Gospel accounts preaching, teaching, healing and walking on the land and sea of Galilee. And that is the other salient truth of the revelation of the glory of God in Jesus – He is very immanent, that is, He is God with us like He was with His followers in Galilee. To truly know Jesus is to know both His sovereignty and His personal closeness.

Jesus is clearly revealed in Scripture as our imminent God, personally close to each one of His children and worthy of our faith, hope, and love. As our God, Jesus became a man and lived among us (John 1:1 and 14), loved us (John 15:12), sacrificed Himself for us (Mark 10:45; Luke 19:10), and promised to always be with us (Matthew 28:19-20).

It is wonderful to realize that the same Jesus, who is the sacrificed Lamb of God, is also our good shepherd. Jesus said, "I am the good shepherd; the good shepherd lays down his life for the sheep" (John 10:11). King David knew the Lord personally as "my shepherd" and described for us what it meant to him to have the Lord as his shepherd and to follow the Lord through his life on *paths of righteousness.*

We will conclude our glimpse of the glory of God revealed in Jesus with a brief look at one of the best known and most loved passages of scripture in the Bible. Psalm 23 is King David's song about following the Lord, his shepherd, throughout his life on *paths of righteousness.*

King David sang:

> The LORD is my shepherd; I shall not want.
> He maketh me to lie down in green pastures;
> He leadeth me beside the still waters.
> He restoreth my soul;
> He leadeth me in the paths of righteousness for his name's sake.
> Yea, though I walk through the valley of the shadow of death, I will fear no evil: for thou art with me;
> Thy rod and thy staff they comfort me.
> Thou preparest a table before me in the presence of mine enemies;
> Thou anointest my head with oil;
> My cup runneth over.
> Surely goodness and mercy shall follow me all the days of my life; and I will dwell in the house of the LORD for ever.

Psalm 23 (KJV)

This song of David begins with a tremendous promise: "I shall not want." Why? "The Lord is my shepherd." Because the

Lord is my shepherd, I shall not want. But I do want. I want lots of things. Even if we understand want in the sense of lack, which I believe is the correct sense here, I can still say that there are things I lack. If I lack, does that mean the Lord is not my shepherd? No. The text says, because the Lord is my shepherd, there are four things that I will not lack.

Because the Lord is my shepherd, "He maketh me to lie down in green pastures." For me, the operative word here is *green*. Green is the color of renewal in the spring. Green is the color of life. Green is the color of growth. Green is the color that promises the hope of a harvest and God's provision from the earth. Anyone who lives close to the earth, including a sheep, instinctively knows the difference between a green pasture and a brown pasture. "He maketh me to lie down in green pastures." My shepherd gives me a resting place where there is renewal, life, growth, and the promise of God's provision for me. Because the Lord is my shepherd, I shall not want for green pastures.

Because the Lord is my shepherd, "He leadeth me beside the still waters." "Still waters" speak to me of refreshment. In contrast to a parched, dry land, my shepherd leads me beside still waters. To the flock, still waters signify refreshment found in safety and security. Still waters also speak of quiet and restfulness, of refreshment found in peace. My shepherd leads me to a place of refreshment in safety; security; and quiet, restful peace. Because the Lord is my shepherd, I shall not be in want of green pastures or still waters.

Because the Lord is my shepherd, "He restoreth my soul; He leadeth me in the *paths of righteousness* for his name's sake." The condition of his flock is a reflection on the shepherd. For the sake of His name, my Shepherd leads me in the "*paths of righteousness*" through green pastures, beside still waters, to restoration. The paths to restoration of the soul are "*paths of righteousness.*" Because the Lord is my shepherd, for the sake of His name, He leads me in the "*paths of righteousness*" through green pastures, beside still waters, to restoration. Because the Lord is my shepherd, I shall not want for green pastures, still waters, His leading or restoration.

But as you may already know, the "*paths of righteousness*" do not end at restoration. Yea though I walk, that is, even though right now we all are walking through the valley of the shadow of death, "I will fear no evil." Even though all around me right now, I see sin and the consequences of sin—separation, suffering, and death—"I will fear no evil." Why? "For thou art with me." For the sake of Your name, You lead me in the "*paths of righteousness*" and when I am following You where You lead, I am with you and "thou art with me."

I would like you to notice what the text does not say. The text does not say, "Yea, though I walk through the valley of the shadow of death, I will experience no evil." It says, "Yea, though I walk through the valley of the shadow of death, I will fear no evil." While following my Shepherd in the "*paths of righteousness*," even though I experience sin and the consequences of sin all around me, I need fear no evil, "for thou art with me." Although the text does not say this, it is my observation that the time to fear evil is when I stray from the "*paths of righteousness.*"

While following You in the "*paths of righteousness*," Your rod and staff comfort me. At times, You may use Your rod and staff to defend and protect me. At other times, when I stray from following You, You may use Your rod and staff on me to discipline me and to bring me back to the "*paths of righteousness.*" At both times, "Thy rod and thy staff they comfort me."

While following You in the "*paths of righteousness,*" "Thou preparest a table before me in the presence of mine enemies." Even with sin, separation and suffering all around me in the valley of the shadow of death, You take care of me and provide for my needs.

Later in his life, David could look back and say, "This people did not anoint me as their king" (Judah in 2 Samuel 2:1-4; all the tribes of Israel in 2 Samuel 5:1-3). "Samuel may have poured the oil, but Samuel did not anoint me as king" (1 Samuel 16:1-13). "Thou anointest my head with oil." You, Lord, anointed me and made me king (Psalm 89:20). You, my Shepherd, have led me every step of the way and have kept bringing me back to the "*paths of righteousness.*" You are the One that brought me to the place in which I stand before You today.

As I look back at the way You have brought me, when I see that You have comforted me with your rod and staff, provided for me in the presence of my enemies, and led me, "my cup runneth over." Even when sin and its consequences—separation and suffering—cast the shadow of death across the "*paths of righteousness,*" You were with me. You protected me and disciplined me to keep me in the "*paths of righteousness.*" You provided for me even when the paths were difficult in the presence of my enemies. You led me every step of the way to the place I now stand before You. Looking back at the "*paths of righteousness*" where You led me, "My cup runneth over" with Your comfort and provision along the way.

Based on Your faithfulness and Your leading in the past, I look forward, trusting You. "Surely goodness and mercy shall follow me all the days of my life," and beyond. Seeing how You have brought me to this point, I trust You to bring me home, "and I will dwell in the house of the Lord for ever."

As a good shepherd, Jesus our Savior, who is the Lord our God (John 20:28-29), is with us and close to us every day, lovingly providing for us and leading us on paths of righteousness that restore our souls. Even when the consequences of sin cast the shadow of death across our path, Jesus is there to protect us, discipline us, comfort us, and provide for our needs. All of us who believe in Jesus and who are following Jesus on the paths of righteousness can look back on our own lives and see that it was Jesus who drew us to Himself. Surely Jesus will continue to shower His children with His goodness and mercy all the days of our lives as He brings us safely home to be with Him forever.

It is my hope and prayer that you will know Jesus and the power of His resurrection, and that you will follow Him on paths of righteousness. I do not know your name yet, but I am praying for you. Hold on tight to Jesus, as He has laid hold of you. Forget what lies behind and reach forward to what lies ahead with Jesus. (See Paul's testimony in Philippians 3:8-14.)

I wish I had a quick, easy method and explanation of how to walk with Jesus on *paths of righteousness*, but I know of none. It is not quick or easy, but begin to carefully read the entire Bible for yourself. Try starting with the New Testament in the Bible and reading about the life of Jesus. As you read through the New Testament, pray every day and ask Jesus to show you in His word how to live and to walk with Him. Also begin this week to meet together in church every week to worship Jesus with others who believe in Jesus. (Hebrews 10:23-25) Look for a church that teaches the Bible and loves Jesus. You will find in church not perfect righteousness, but the companionship and the encouragement of following Jesus with brothers and sisters who, like you and me, also need continual forgiveness and encouragement. Ask them and ask the pastor your questions about the Bible and your life, get involved with them in church activities, and follow Jesus with them on the *paths of righteousness*.

May you truly know Jesus as your God and follow Him throughout your life as your personal shepherd and companion on *paths of righteousness*.

> Now the God of peace, who brought up from the dead the great Shepherd of the sheep through the blood of the eternal covenant, even Jesus our Lord, equip you in every good thing to do His will, working in us that which is pleasing in His sight, through Jesus Christ, to whom be the *glory* forever and ever. Amen.
>
> Hebrews 13.20-21 (italics mine)

Behold His glory.

THE GIFT OF GOD

In the preceding pages, I have emphasized Scripture that explains our responsibility and freedom to respond in faith to the gospel, to the word of reconciliation, and to Jesus Christ. This is in no way intended to diminish what the Bible teaches about the grace and sovereignty of God, which is clearly presented in Scripture.

For an adequate treatment of God's sovereign grace in His work of salvation, I must leave you at this time to consult Scripture for yourself. I will offer this observation only as a starting point.

> For by grace you have been saved through faith; and that not of yourselves, it is *the gift of God*; not as a result of works, so that no one may boast.
>
> Ephesians 2:8-9 (italics mine)

Notice that salvation is something that is done to us by God, "you have been saved"; not something we do for ourselves, "not as a result of works"; and not something for which we can take any credit, "that no one may boast."

The means of salvation is described by two phrases in this text. Salvation is "by grace" and "through faith." I have purposefully emphasized the "through faith" aspect of salvation in this document because there is no doubt in my mind that God is faithful. The question is, are we? God will complete His sovereign purpose "by grace." Will we respond to Him "through faith"?

It is clear in Scripture that salvation is something God gives to us by His sovereign grace. We are predestined and called according to His purpose, not ours (Romans 8:28-32; 2 Timothy 1:8-9). "God's grace," that is, "God's benefit bestowed on the unworthy," is at the heart of the Promise of God, the Gospel of God, the Works of God, Reconciliation with God, the Will of God, and the Revelation of God as Jesus Christ.

Our salvation is "*the gift of God.*"

> He who did not spare His own Son, but delivered Him over for us all, how will He not also with Him freely give us all things?
>
> Romans 8:32

> Thanks be to God for His indescribable gift!
>
> 2 Corinthians 9.15

For by grace you have been saved.

Behold His glory.

GLOSSARY OF BIBLICAL TERMS

Faith: agreement + assurance + commitment

Faith is agreement with, confidence in, and commitment to a person, truth, or command that lead to a response. Doubt is disagreement or ambivalence that leads to being unresponsive.

Faith is a response involving agreement with content, assurance of effectiveness, and personal commitment.

Discussion: Biblical faith involves content. It does not just say, "I believe." Biblical faith says, "I believe *in* something or someone." Biblical faith involves agreement with a body of content, plus assurance or conviction of the effectiveness of that content, plus a personal commitment, a response of trust to the truth of the content.

Saving faith is:

> agreement that Jesus is God the Son who died on a cross and rose from the dead.

assurance that He died *for me*. Assurance is personal. It involves acknowledgement and confession of who and what I am before the Lord and conviction that the content of faith applies to me and is effective for me. Knowing *me*, Jesus died *for me*.

commitment to Jesus. In submission to Jesus, faith is trusting only in His death for me and His righteousness to be reconciled with God and healed.

Example of faith: Suppose four men on a ship fall overboard and someone throws each one a life preserver.

The first man disagrees that it is a life preserver and does not take hold of it. "This is no life preserver." Without agreement about the content, the object of faith, his faith is incomplete and he drowns.

The second man agrees that it is a life preserver, but has no assurance it can help him, so he does not take hold of it. "This is a life preserver, but it won't help me." Without assurance that the content, the object, is effective for him, His faith is incomplete and he drowns.

The third man agrees that it is a life preserver and has confidence that it can help him, but he decides not to take hold of it. "This is a life preserver. It can help me, but I will not depend on it." Agreement about the object, or content, and assurance that it is effective is not enough. Unless he grabs hold and depends on it, his faith is incomplete and he drowns.

The fourth man agrees that it is a life preserver and that it can help him, and he commits himself and takes hold of it. "This is a life preserver. It will help me, and I trust it." His faith is complete, and he is saved.[13]

See also *hope*.

> *Glory*: Glory is that which weighs, demonstrates, declares, verifies, or authenticates the identity, nature, value, or worth of an object or person.

To glorify is to weigh, demonstrate, declare, verify, or authenticate the identity, nature, value, or worth of an object or person.

Discussion: The literal sense of the Hebrew word *glory* has to do with weight. An object in a market was weighed to confirm or verify what it was and to determine its value. An object's glory, its weight in the balance, authenticated what it was and demonstrated its value. An action or statement that glorifies God is one that shows who God is and declares that He is worthy of our worship, obedience, faith, hope, and love.

> *Grace*: a blessing or benefit bestowed on the *undeserving*.

Discussion: The recipient of an act of grace says, "I do not deserve this. I am not worthy of this act."

See *mercy*.

Hope: agreement + assurance + commitment

Hope is agreement with, confidence in, and commitment to a person, truth, or *promise* that lead to a response. Doubt is disagreement or ambivalence that leads to being unresponsive.

Hope is a response involving agreement with content, assurance of effectiveness, and personal commitment.

A response of hope to a person, truth, or promise is essentially the same as a response of faith. A response of hope generally looks forward into the future but can involve the present. Although a faith response has a more present implication, it also looks forward.

See *faith*.

Mercy: a blessing or benefit bestowed on the *helpless*.

Discussion: The recipient of an act of mercy says, "I cannot do this. I am helpless without this act."

See *grace*.

ENDNOTES

1   R. Laird Harris, Gleason L. Archer and Bruce K. Waltke, *Theological Wordbook of the Old Testament*, Moody Press, Chicago, IL, 1980, article titled "כבד", Volume 1, pp 426-428.

2   *Archaeology and the Old Testament*, Merrill F. Unger, Zondervan Publishing House, Grand Rapids, Michigan, 1954, pp 267 – 270.

3   This was the opinion of Dr. Samuel Schultz that he expressed in class to his students; reference *Archaeology and the Old Testament*, Merrill F. Unger, Zondervan Publishing House, Grand Rapids, Michigan, 1954, pp 282 – 284; see also *The Old Testament Speaks*, Samuel J Schultz, Harper & Row, Publishers, New York and Evanston, 1960, pp 224-225.

4   *The Zondervan Pictorial Encyclopedia of the Bible*, Merrill C. Tenney, General Editor, The Zondervan Corporation, Grand Rapids, Michigan, 1975, article titled "Temple, Jerusalem," p. 622ff.

5   See also 2 Kings 16:5-6 and 2 Kings 25:25. It appears the term *Jew* originally referred to those from the tribe of Judah, as opposed to members from one of the other tribes of Israel.

6   Aspects of the suffering of Jesus on the cross sung about in Psalm 22:

Psalm 22:1 "My God, my God, why have You forsaken me?" (Matthew 27:46, Mark 15:34).

Psalm 22:7-8 "All who see me sneer at me…they wag the head" (Matthew 27:39-40, Mark 15:19-20), "saying, 'Commit yourself to the Lord; let Him deliver him; let Him rescue him, because He delights in him'" (Matthew 27:41-43).

Psalm 22:16 "They pierced my hands and my feet" (John 20:19-28).

Psalm 22:18 "They divide my garments among them, and for my clothing they cast lots" (Matthew 27:35; Luke 23:34; John 19:23-24).

The disciples remembered Psalm 69:9 as a reference to Jesus.

Psalm 69:9 "For zeal for Your house has consumed me, and the reproaches of those who reproach You have fallen on me" (John 2:15-17).

The reign of the Lord's anointed one, that is, the Messiah, the Christ is sung about in Psalm 2.

Psalm 2:1-3 "The LORD and…His Anointed."

Psalm 2:4-6 "I have installed My King upon Zion, My holy mountain."

Psalm 2:7-9 "You are My Son, today I have begotten You. Ask of Me, and I will surely give the nations as Your inheritance, and the very ends of the earth as Your possession."

Psalm 2:10-12 "Worship the LORD with reverence… Do homage to the Son."

Jesus quoted this prayer of David in Psalm 110 and asked a question:

Psalm 110:1 "The LORD says to my Lord: 'Sit at My right hand until I make Your enemies a footstool for Your feet.'"

Luke 20:41-44 "Then He (*Jesus*) said to them, 'How is it that they say the Christ is David's son? For David himself says in the book of Psalms, "The Lord said to my Lord, 'Sit at my right hand, until I make your enemies a footstool for your feet.'" Therefore David calls Him "Lord," and how is He his son?" (italics mine).

David sang a song about the Lord God referring to Messiah, the One sitting at the right hand of God, as David's Lord. "If David called Messiah his Lord," Jesus asked, "how can David's Lord also be David's son?" In other words, who really existed first, David or Christ the Messiah?

Peter interpreted Psalm 110 as referring to Jesus:

Acts 2:32-36 "This Jesus God raised up again, to which we are all witnesses...For it was not David who ascended into heaven, but he himself says: 'The Lord said to my Lord, sit at my right hand, until I make your enemies a footstool for your feet.' Therefore let all the house of Israel know for certain that God has made Him both Lord and Christ—this Jesus whom you crucified."

Peter preached from Psalm 110 that the Lord God Himself made Jesus to be both Lord/God and Messiah/Christ, this same Jesus that you crucified.

Psalms 110:4 "The LORD has sworn and will not change His mind, 'You are a priest forever...'"

The Lord God Himself has also established Messiah Jesus as a priest forever, that is, as our eternal intercessor before God.

7   Isaiah 7:14 "A virgin will be with child and bear a son, and she will call His name Immanuel."

"The Lord will give you a sign—a virgin will have a child who will be called Immanuel, which means 'God with us.'" (Matthew 1:18-25; Luke 1:26-35).

Isaiah 35:4-6 "Say to those with anxious heart, 'Take courage, fear not. Behold, your God will come...' Then the eyes of the blind will be opened and the ears of the deaf will be unstopped. Then the lame will leap like a deer, and the tongue of the mute will shout for joy."

When God Himself comes to you, look for these signs: the blind will see; the deaf will hear; the lame will leap; the mute will shout. (Matthew 9:35, Mark 7:33-35, John 5:5-9).

Jeremiah 31:14-15 "And My people will be satisfied with My goodness," declares the LORD. Thus says the LORD, "A voice is heard in Ramah, lamentation and bitter weeping. Rachel is weeping for her children; she refuses to be comforted for her children, because they are no more."

"At the time My people are satisfied with My goodness,"declared the Lord, "there will also be a slaughter of children" (Matthew 2:16).

Micah 5:2-4 "But as for you, Bethlehem Ephrathah, too little to be among the clans of Judah, from you One will go forth for Me to be ruler in Israel. His goings forth are from long ago, from the days of eternity."

When the magi arrived seeking the One born King of the Jews, Herod gathered the chief priests and scribes to ask them where Messiah was to be born (Matthew 2:1-6).

Zechariah 9:9 "Rejoice greatly, O daughter of Zion! Shout in triumph, O daughter of Jerusalem! Behold, your king is coming to you; He is just and endowed with salvation, humble, and mounted on a donkey, even on a colt, the foal of a donkey.

When Messiah comes to Jerusalem as your King to bring you salvation, he will arrive mounted on the colt of a donkey" (Luke 19:29-38).

Zechariah 11:12-13 "I said to them, 'If it is good in your sight, give me my wages; but if not, never mind!' So they weighed out thirty shekels of silver as my wages. Then the LORD said to me, 'Throw it to the potter, that magnificent price at which I was valued by them.' So I took the thirty shekels of silver and threw them to the potter in the house of the LORD.

The Lord called thirty pieces of silver the "price at which I was valued by them," and told the prophet to throw the silver "to the potter in the house of the LORD," which is what happened (Matthew 26:14-15 and 27:3-7).

Zechariah 12:10 "They will look on Me whom they have pierced; and they will mourn for Him, as one mourns for an only son, and they will weep bitterly over Him like the bitter weeping over a firstborn."

The Lord said that one day the house of David "will look on Me whom they have pierced," and they will mourn for me; "as one mourns for an only son" (John 19:34-37 and 3:16).

Malachi 3:1 "The Lord, whom you seek, will suddenly come to His temple…"

Jesus did come to the temple, which He referred to as "My house" (Matthew 21:12-13).

8   The Hebrew name given to Jesus was a sentence name. A more literal translation than "Savior" might be "He Saves." You shall call His name "He Saves," for it is He who will save. See *Theological Dictionary of the New Testament*, Gerhard Kittel, WM. B. Eerdmans Publishing Company, Grand Rapids, Michigan, 1965, Volume III, article titled "Ἰησοῦς", p 284ff. See also Volume VII, article titled "σώζω", p 965ff.

9   As a spoken message, the Hebrew stem, בשׂר, used as a verb here, would have the sense of "proclaiming good news" or "bringing news of victory." The written Greek verb used here is εὐαγγελίζομαι, which is translated by the English phrase, "I bring good news." It has the sense of one who "speaks as" or "acts like" a messenger of good news. This Hebrew stem used as a noun has the sense of "good news" to the hearer. The effective power of the message demands or causes a response of joy; it effects what it proclaims. The Greek noun εὐαγγέλιον has the sense

of "good news" or "news of victory" to the one who hears the messenger. See *Theological Dictionary of the New Testament*, Gerhard Kittel, WM. B. Eerdmans Publishing Company, Grand Rapids, Michigan, 1964, Volume II, article titled "εὐαγγελίζομαι", p 707ff.

10   See C S Lewis's *Mere Christianity*, Macmillan Publishing Co., Inc., 1952, especially his chapter entitled "The Shocking Alternative," pp. 51-56; see also McDowell, Josh, *More Than A Carpenter*, Tyndale House Publishers, Inc, Wheaton, Illinois, 1977, especially his chapter entitled "Lord, Liar or Lunatic," pp 25-35.

11   It is instructive to consider how the early church used and understood this phrase, "the revelation of Jesus Christ."

Paul wrote: "You are…awaiting eagerly *the revelation of our Lord Jesus Christ*, who will also confirm you to the end, blameless in the day of our Lord Jesus Christ (1 Corinthians 1:7-8; see 1:4-8; italics mine).

What the church in Corinth was eagerly awaiting was not a new message from Jesus, but His return, His revealing at "the end." "*The Revelation of Jesus Christ*" to this church meant the day of the return of Jesus, "the day of our Lord Jesus Christ," the day Jesus would be revealed at "the end" of time.

Peter wrote to Christians residing as aliens in the world: "Blessed be the God and Father of our Lord Jesus Christ, who according to His great mercy has caused us to be born again to a living hope through the resurrection of Jesus Christ from the dead, to obtain an inheritance which is imperishable and undefiled and will not fade away, reserved in heaven for you, who are protected by the power of God through faith for a salvation ready to be revealed in the last time. In this you greatly rejoice, even though now for a little while, if necessary, you have been distressed by various trials, so that the proof of your faith, being more precious than gold which is perishable, even though tested by fire, may be found to result in praise and glory and honor at *the revelation of Jesus Christ*" (1 Peter 1:3-7; italics mine).

What these believers were waiting for was "a salvation ready to be revealed in the last time." To the early church, the phrase, "*the revelation of Jesus Christ,*" was not about a new message from Jesus, but rather the revealing of Jesus after "a little while" when He would return and bring an imperishable inheritance reserved in heaven for them.

12   In the order in which they appear in "The Revelation of Jesus Christ," the following verses describe the *worship* of demons, idols, the dragon and the beast, and the final end of worshiping these false gods:

"The rest of mankind, who were not killed by these plagues, did not repent of the works of their hands, so as not to *worship* demons, and the idols of gold and of silver and of brass and of stone and of wood, which can neither see nor hear nor walk; and they did not repent of their murders nor of their sorceries nor of their immorality nor of their thefts" (Revelation 9:20-21; italics mine).

"And the whole earth was amazed and followed after the beast; they *worshiped* the dragon because he gave his authority to the beast; and they *worshiped* the beast, saying, 'Who is like the beast, and who is able to wage war with him?'" Revelation 13:3-4; italics mine).

"All who dwell on the earth will *worship* him, everyone whose name has not been written from the foundation of the world in the book of life of the Lamb who has been slain. If anyone has an ear, let him hear. If anyone is destined for captivity, to captivity he goes; if anyone kills with the sword, with the sword he must be killed. Here is the perseverance and the faith of the saints" (Revelation 13:8-10; italics mine).

"Then I saw another beast coming up out of the earth; and he had two horns like a lamb and he spoke as a dragon. He exercises all the authority of the first beast in his presence. And he makes the earth and those who dwell in it to *worship* the first beast, whose fatal wound was healed" (Revelation 13:11-12; italics mine).

"And it was given to him to give breath to the image of the beast, so that the image of the beast would even speak and cause as many as do not *worship* the image of the beast to be killed" (Revelation 13:15; italics mine).

"And the smoke of their torment goes up forever and ever; they have no rest day and night, those who *worship* the beast and his image, and whoever receives the mark of his name" (Revelation 14:11; italics mine).

"So the first angel went and poured out his bowl on the earth; and it became a loathsome and malignant sore on the people who had the mark of the beast and who *worshiped* his image" (Revelation 16:2; italics mine).

"And the beast was seized, and with him the false prophet who performed the signs in his presence, by which he deceived those who had received the mark of the beast and those who *worshiped* his image; these two were thrown alive into the lake of fire which burns with brimstone" (Revelation 19:20; italics mine).

13 Acknowledgement to Larry Moyer of EvanTell, Inc., PO Box 741417, Dallas, TX 75374, for the concept and general content of this example.